NEW HODDER English Gold

3

Sue Hackman &
Alan Howe

Hodder & Stoughton

A MEMBER OF THE HODDER HEADLINE GROUP

ACKNOWLEDGEMENTS

The publishers would like to thank the following contributors:

Paul Siebert and Adrian Jones	- *Unit One, *Stone Cold*
John Rowley and David Watkinson	- *Unit Two, *Newsroom*
Karen Blake and Lynette Newman	- *Unit Three, *Macbeth*
Jo Shackleton	- Unit Four, *Getting Ready for the National Tests*
Andrew McCallum	- Unit Five, *Black British Poetry*
John Rowley and Dave Watkinson	- *Unit Six, *Scandal*
Jo Shackleton	- *Unit Seven, *What the Dickens!*

* These units have been revised by Sue Hackman and Alan Howe.

Copyright text:
pp 17, 18, 22, 24, 32, 33 from *Stone Cold* © Robert Swindells, Penguin; p25 from the BBC TV 'Scene' adaptation of *Stone Cold* © BBC Worldwide Ltd; p112 *Tropical Death* by Grace Nichols © Time Warner Books, *The Fat Black Woman Goes Shopping* by Grace Nichols © Time Warner Books; p113 *Beauty* by Grace Nichols © Time Warner Books; p114 *De Generation Rap* by Benjamin Zephaniah © Viking, Puffin; p116 *Checking Out Me History* by John Agard © Viking, Puffin, *The British* by Benjamin Zephaniah © Viking, Puffin; p119 *Tessa* from 'Get Back Pimples' published by Viking, Puffin 1996, by John Agard reproduced with kind permission of John Agard c/o Caroline Sheldon literary agency; p120 *Rainbow* by John Agard from 'Mangoes and Bullets' © John Agard 1985, published by Serpent's Tail; p161 *Sons and Lovers* by D.H. Lawrence © Penguin, first published by Penguin in 1948, previously published in 1913, *Flour Babies* by Anne Fine © Puffin, 1992.

Copyright photographs:
p20 [top, left] © Peter Dunkley/Life File, [middle] © Andrew Ward/Life File, [right] Jeremy Hoare/Life File, [bottom, left] © Alan Smith/Tony Stone, [middle] © Andrew Ward/Life File, [right] © David Kampfner/Colorific!; pp25, 26, 27, 30 © Luke Finn/BBC Education by kind permission of the producer Andy Rowley, for 'Scene'; p35 [top] © Photo Press, [bottom] © Photo Press; p44 all photographs © Hodder & Stoughton; p45 [clockwise from top] © Tony Stone, © JT Turner/Telegraph Colour Library, © Ed Horn/Telegraph Colour Library, © N Battersby; p48 © Hodder & Stoughton; p85 © Donald Cooper/Photostage; p87 © Donald Cooper/Photostage; p88 © Donald Cooper/Photostage; p89 © Donald Cooper/Photostage; p110 © Michael Nicholson/CORBIS; p113 © Gillian Cargill/Little Brown publishers; p114 © Bloodaxe books; p118 © Hodder & Stoughton; pp143, 146, 150, 159, 164, 165, 166, 167, 168 © The Dickens House Museum.

Copyright artwork:
Cover: Darren Hopes
Internals: Kate Sardella of Ian Foulis & Associates

Every effort has been made to trace copyright holders of material reproduced in this book. Any rights not acknowledged here will be acknowledged in subsequent printings if notice is given to the publisher.

Order queries: please contact Bookpoint Ltd, 130 Milton Park, Abingdon, Oxon OX14 4SB.
Telephone: (44) 01235 827720, Fax (44) 01235 400454. Lines are open from 9.00 - 6.00, Monday to Saturday, with a 24 hour message answering service. Email address: orders@bookpoint.co.uk
You can also order through our website at www.hodderheadline.co.uk

British Library Cataloguing in Publication Data
A catalogue record for this title is available from The British Library

ISBN 0 340 84657 7

First published 2002
Impression number   10   9   8   7   6   5   4   3   2
Year   2006   2005   2004   2003

Copyright © 2002 Sue Hackman and Alan Howe

Designed and typeset by Mind's Eye Design, Lewes.

Printed in Italy for Hodder & Stoughton Educational, a division of Hodder Headline, 338 Euston Road, London NW1 3BH.

INTRODUCTION

Welcome to *New Hodder English Gold,* which comprises three fully-revised editions of books in the *Hodder English Gold* series. This course book and its two companions represent a quality English curriculum for pupils working at levels 2–4 in Key Stage 3 (S1–3). It has been planned and written to meet the demands of Key Stage 3 Strategy framework for teaching English in years 7, 8 and 9, to cover the National Curriculum (and Scottish 5–14 Guidelines) and to maintain a challenging, vigorous and progressive ethos in the classroom. Book 1 introduces pupils to a wide and challenging variety of English experiences and assignments, which are then progressively built on and broadened in *New Hodder English Gold 2* and *3.* However, teachers may wish to use these books to supplement their own schemes of work, or other materials.

RAISING STANDARDS AND COVERING NATIONAL CURRICULUM REQUIREMENTS

We have taken as our prime directive the advancement of pupil learning. All the materials in *New Hodder English Gold* have been trialled in the classroom by English teachers to offer the very best of current practice. Units have been developed to address the objectives in the English Framework, to cover the National Curriculum in England, Wales and Northern Ireland and the 5–14 Guidelines in Scotland. At the same time, we know that pupils in the early levels of literacy need explicit instruction and scaffolded activities. We have provided both in the context of purposeful work and quality texts. Each book contains one unit of work that addresses basic skills as a focus of work in its own right and consolidation activities have been built in later.

New Hodder English Gold addresses the appropriate number of set texts and includes many more. Pre-twentieth century literature is amply represented in both fiction and non-fiction. You will find here a catholic range of genres, tones and forms, but we have resisted simplified versions in favour of abridgement. We have made particular efforts to ensure that speaking and listening is fully represented in the series, not merely as incidental group talk but as a purposeful activity in its own right.

STRUCTURE

New Hodder English Gold consists of three books, one for each year at Key Stage 3 (years S1–3 in Scotland) and a CD. Each book is divided into units, which have been arranged across the three years to establish, revisit and consolidate key skills.

Although the units have been placed in an order which offers pupils a varied and progressive experience of English, you can use the book in a flexible way, linking units with others or with texts you want to teach.

Whilst we have introduced basic skills directly through key units, and again in the context of others, we also assume that teachers will continue to support individual pupils by giving them feedback on their oral and written performance, and that spelling, punctuation and grammar will be part of this continuing work.

It is strongly recommended that the *New Hodder English Gold* books are complemented by the use of *Hodder Starters,* to ensure that word and sentence level objectives are fully and explicitly addressed.

PROGRESSION

New Hodder English Gold 1, 2, and *3* form an incremental programme of work with clear goals written with the expressed intention of raising standards in English. The course offers far more than a sequence of self-contained lessons or starting points because progression is built into each unit, between each book and across the course as a whole. Key elements of English are focused on once in each year, and incidentally as a part of other units.

ASSESSMENT

Assessment is an integral part of each unit. However, checklists, recording sheets and assessment grids are deliberately not included, as it is most likely that you have already developed a workable system. Teaching by units enables you to collect evidence of pupils' achievements periodically, and systematically, at the end of each unit. The book provides the pupils with focused tasks and explicit criteria for evaluating how well they are doing, and what they need to improve on.

ACTIVITIES

The initial material and activities of each unit are designed to introduce pupils to the focus for the sequence of work, and to engage their interest. There is then a series of tasks designed to help pupils to develop specific areas of knowledge, understanding and skill. Several pages are given to consolidating new knowledge or skills in context.

USING *NEW HODDER ENGLISH GOLD*

Many of the units are free-standing and teachers will find them sufficiently flexible to introduce extra material or to extend their use beyond a half-term. Texts have been chosen for their quality and for their richness in classroom study, as well as for their accessibility, and relevance for the age group. Where it has been impractical to reproduce whole texts, we have produced extracts to support the close study of key passages.

In addition, the CD provides support where it is most helpful. To promote reading skills, we recommend that pupils conduct close study activities using the text as well as the CD so that they can learn how to find particular words, phrases and information in the text. Where icon **A** appears (see below), either on its own or as icon **C** (see below), the text which is being studied is provided on the CD as well.

For your convenience, a number of pages have been designed as *photocopiable*. These pages contain activities which pupils will do best if they are involved in hands-on work.

A

Text provided
on CD.

B

Task, involving
reading, writing
and/or drama.

C

Task, involving
reading, writing
and/or drama.
Related text is
provided on CD.

CONTENTS

MAPPING GRIDS

The following mapping grids show which English Framework objectives for Year 9 are addressed in each unit.

READING	UNIT ONE: STONE COLD	UNIT TWO: NEWSROOM	UNIT THREE: MACBETH	UNIT FOUR: GETTING READY FOR NATIONAL TESTS	UNIT FIVE: BLACK BRITISH POETRY	UNIT SIX: SCANDAL	UNIT SEVEN: WHAT THE DICKENS!
1				✔			
2		✔					
3				✔		✔	
4							
5				✔			
6					✔		✔
7						✔	
8		✔				✔	
9							✔
10	✔						
11	✔	✔				✔	✔
12							✔
13					✔		
14			✔				
15			✔				✔
16					✔		
17					✔		
18	✔						

	UNIT ONE: STONE COLD	UNIT TWO: NEWSROOM	UNIT THREE: MACBETH	UNIT FOUR: GETTING READY FOR NATIONAL TESTS	UNIT FIVE: BLACK BRITISH POETRY	UNIT SIX: SCANDAL	UNIT SEVEN: WHAT THE DICKENS!
SPEAKING AND LISTENING							
1						✔	
2	✔	✔					
3		✔					
4						✔	
5		✔			✔	✔	
6		✔				✔	
7						✔	
8						✔	
9						✔	
10	✔	✔			✔	✔	
11			✔				
12	✔		✔				
13			✔				
14	✔						
15			✔				

TEACHER GUIDANCE

READING		WRITING		SPEAKING & LISTENING	
10	Interpretations of text	2	Exploratory writing	2	Standard English
11	Author's standpoint	13	Influence audience	10	Group organisation
18	Prose text	14	Counter-argument	12	Drama techniques
		15	Impartial guidance	14	Convey characters and atmosphere

TEACHING SEQUENCE

The suggested sequence anticipates that you will use the unit as the basis for a 'staged' reading of the whole novel with the class, using the materials in *New Hodder Gold 3* as the basis for focused discussion and activities that will gradually build up and deepen pupils' response as they go along.

Week 1:	Introduction to the author, key themes in the novel. Begin novel and read up to the end of Daily Routine Orders 4; first impressions, reading log.
Week 2:	Up to end of Daily Routine Orders 9; characters and relationships.
Week 3:	Up to end of Daily Routine Orders 13; plot and narrative technique.
Week 4:	Read to end of novel; Shelter; horror; ending and overview.
Week 5:	Writing to argue and advise.

TEACHERS' NOTES

This award-winning novel by Robert Swindells explores the experience of homelessness in a fictional story that becomes increasingly mysterious and ultimately horrific. A particular feature of the novel is the use of dual narrators. The novel will provide Year 9 pupils with an accessible text that is also challenging both in its content and narrative devices. As the teaching sequence above illustrates, we suggest planning to teach the novel in a series of weekly lessons focusing on key sections and teaching objectives, using the materials in the unit as key stopping off points. Pupils are asked to keep a 'Reading Log' as they progress through the novel as a way of catching their ideas and developing a written response to key episodes: this works best if you can develop a dialogue with pupils in their log prompting reflection by asking questions and recording, briefly, your own ideas and responses. Extend and enhance the unit by gathering a collection of other Robert Swindells novels such as *Brother in the Land* and *Daz 4 Zoe*.

UNIT TWO: NEWSROOM

READING	WRITING	SPEAKING & LISTENING
2 Synthesise information	4 Presentational devices	2 Standard English
8 Readers and texts	9 Integrate information	3 Interview techniques
11 Author's standpoint	12 Effective presentation of information	5 Compare points of view
	13 influence audience	6 Analyse bias
	16 Balanced analysis	10 Group organisation

TEACHING SEQUENCE

Lessons 1–2:	A story breaks
Lessons 3–4:	Putting a story together (Later that day, Picture Power, Headlines and Layout)
Lesson 5–7:	Writing and presenting the news (Writing the News, Unscrambling the News and Reading the News)
Lessons 8–12:	Hijack story

TEACHERS' NOTES

You can build a topical and interesting unit by collecting up interesting newspaper covers and television bulletins in the weeks prior to teaching this unit.

Lessons 1–2: Note that you will need a number of newspapers for one of the activities. Organise pupils into groups with at least one copy per pupil. You could reproduce this activity using yesterday's stories from the short early evening TV news, and ask pupils to put them in order before showing the outcome.

Lessons 3–4: Good starters for these lessons would include wall displays of recent front pages with pictures or headlines blocked out with plain paper. Pupils could speculate what would appear in these blanks before showing the originals. Collect up front pages which feature striking images.

Lessons 5–7: You will need a video camera and a quiet setting for recording the news.

Lessons 8–12: Aim to cover a bulletin each lesson, as if in real time. You will need the video camera each lesson, but rotate the recording of the lessons' bulletin among the groups.

UNIT THREE: MACBETH

READING	WRITING	SPEAKING & LISTENING
14 Analyse scenes	16 Balanced analysis	11 Evaluate own drama skills
15 Major writers	17 Cite textual evidence	12 Drama techniques
		13 Compare interpretations
		15 Critical evaluation

TEACHING SEQUENCE

Lesson 1:	Introduction to themes: role play
Lesson 2:	Opening scene
Lessons 3–5:	Act 1; the art of persuasion
Lessons 6–8:	Act 2; investigating the murder
Lessons 9–11:	Act 3; staging the banquet scene
Lessons 12–13:	Act 4
Lessons 14–15:	Act 5
Lessons 16–17:	Groups each focus on a different character
Lesson 18:	Group presentations
Lessons 19–20:	Writing about the play

TEACHERS' NOTES

The unit supports an exploration of the play over a period of approximately half a term. You will need a class set of *Macbeth* so that you can treat the play as a script to be interpreted and explored through a range of drama, role-play and reading activities. Each act in the unit is summarised through using a cartoon version, but we recommend that you support pupils' learning by using a video of the play and the BBC 'Animated Tales' version as well. Use video to introduce a scene, or to accelerate from one closely studied scene to the next. A number of the drama activities will benefit from working in a flexible space. The unit concludes with a series of 'Focus on . . .' study pages which invite pupils to review their understanding of the play by considering key characters; an active way of using these will be to subdivide the class into groups each of whom works on one character, culminating in oral presentations.

UNIT FOUR: GETTING READY FOR NATIONAL TESTS

READING	WRITING	SPEAKING & LISTENING
1 **Information retrieval**	1 Review own writing	
3 Note-making at speed	2 Planning formats	
5 **Evaluate own critical writing**	3 Formal essay	
	6 Creativity in non-literary texts	
	7 'Infotainment'	
	10 Explain connections	
	17 Cite textual evidence	

TEACHING SEQUENCE

Lesson 1:	Introduction
Lessons 2–3:	Tackling reading questions
Lessons 4–5:	Writing a good answer
Lesson 6:	Non-fiction reading
Lessons 7–8:	Planning narrative writing
Lessons 9–10:	Planning non-narrative writing

TEACHERS' NOTES

This unit contains a lot of good advice, but pupils may pass over it. A good approach is to ask pupils in advance what might be in the bullet lists of advice before you read them together, and at the end of the unit, you can ask them at the end to reconstruct the lists from memory.

The short tasks are best tackled in groups, so that the process of finding and shaping answer material is clearly visible. This will help the pupils who stab at an answer without having a methodical way of justifying their views on paper.

Use the groupwork time to join borderline groups to talk them through the process.

To extend this unit:
*   Show examples of real questions on real papers and allow pupils time to plan answers in small groups.
*   Allow time to answer questions as a whole class, so you can model how to marshal materials and how to express and structure answers.
*   Allow pupils to practise individual answers then share ideas, examples and comments in a whole class debriefing.
*   Share mark schemes.
*   Run a mini-moderation based on anonymous past pupil efforts.

The objectives in bold are key objectives that are fully developed in the unit.

UNIT FIVE: BLACK BRITISH POETRY

READING	WRITING	SPEAKING & LISTENING
6 Authorial perspective	8 Poetic form and meaning	5 Compare points of view
13 Evaluate own reading		10 Group organisation
16 Different cultural contexts		
17 Compare poets		

TEACHING SEQUENCE

Lessons 1–3:	Three poems by Grace Nichols
Lesson 4–5:	'De Generation Rap' – focus on language; own poem
Lesson 6–7:	Compare and contrast – John Agard and Benjamin Zephaniah
Lesson 8:	'Tess' – prepared reading aloud
Lesson 9:	'Rainbow' and 'Epilogue'

TEACHERS' NOTES

This unit focuses on a key objective in Year 9: *'Reading 16. Analyse ways in which different cultural contexts and traditions have influenced language and style. e.g. black British poetry, Irish short stories;'* Each section of the unit is designed to build up pupils' appreciation of the distinctive voices that are present in a range of recent black British poetry. The poems selected are all accessible, yet deal with subject matter relevant to Year 9 pupils. We recommend that you use the readings that are available on the tape so that pupils can appreciate the distinctive sound and rhythm, as a preparation for later sections where pupils are encouraged to plan and rehearse their own readings. The most challenging element of the unit is the section asking pupils to compare and contrast the two styles of John Agard and Benjamin Zephaniah; support pupils by giving the opportunities to hear the two poems read aloud several times. The statements activity linked to this section is best carried out in pairs or small groups to encourage maximum discussion and re-reading of the poems.

UNIT SIX: SCANDAL

READING	WRITING	SPEAKING & LISTENING
3 Note-making at speed	2 Exploratory writing	1 Evaluate own talk
7 Compare texts	13 Influence audience	4 Evaluate own listening skills
8 Readers and texts		5 Compare points of view
11 Author's standpoint		6 Analyse bias
		7 Identify underlying issues
		8 Evaluate own contributions
		9 Consider viewpoint
		10 Group organisation

TEACHING SEQUENCE

Lessons 1–3:	Exploring the issues
Lessons 4–5:	Facts and opinions
Lessons 6–7:	Dilemmas
Lessons 8–9:	Review of speaking and listening
Lesson 10:	Contrasting texts

TEACHERS' NOTES

You could develop this unit by:
- comparing treatments of similar stories in different newspapers
- following the development of a major story.

Note the contribution of the sections entitled *Getting your message across* and *What would you do?* to the school's citizenship curriculum.

UNIT SEVEN: WHAT THE DICKENS!

READING	WRITING	SPEAKING & LISTENING
6 Authorial perspective	5 Narrative techniques	
9 Compare writers from different times	11 Descriptive detail	
11 Author's standpoint	17 Cite textual evidence	
12 Rhetorical devices		
15 Major writers		

TEACHING SEQUENCE

Lesson 1:	Dickens' London
Lesson 2:	Dickens captures the reader's attention
Lesson 3:	Pen portraits
Lesson 4:	Naming names
Lesson 5–6:	Dickens paints a picture
Lesson 7:	Goosebumps
Lesson 8–9:	Oliver Twist
Lesson 10:	A grisly end
Lesson 11–12:	Dickens and society

TEACHERS' NOTES

This unit features a number of favourite extracts from Dickens' work. You may well have televised versions available to show the class.

Lesson 1: It would be useful to have slides or illustrations to show.

Lesson 4: Share the pen portraits produced, pointing out effective techniques and praising good efforts.

Lesson 5–6: Demonstrate how to search and annotate descriptive details on an OHT. This will be useful in the tests.

Stone Cold

ROBERT SWINDELLS – A BIOGRAPHY

Stone Cold is a novel about homelessness by Robert Swindells.

Robert Swindells was born in Bradford in 1939. He was the eldest of five children. He left school at 15 and worked on a local newspaper until he was 17, when he joined the RAF. He served for three years in the UK and Germany. After leaving the RAF he had a variety of jobs in factories and offices. Between 1967 and 1969 he took five GCE O-levels at night school. He went to college in 1969 to train as a teacher. While he was at college he wrote a children's novel. It was published in 1973. He worked as a teacher from 1972 to 1980. He wrote in his spare time, and then became a full-time author.

He was an active member of the anti-nuclear movement and he took a master's degree in Peace Studies at the University of Bradford. In 1987 he was jailed for seven days for his part in a CND 'Snowball' non-violent action. Robert has written more than 50 books for young people. He has won a number of awards, including the Carnegie Medal. He is married. He has two grown-up daughters and three grandchildren. He lives on the Yorkshire moors.

WHY I WROTE THE NOVEL

Why did Robert Swindells choose to write a novel on homelessness?
Read the author's own answer to this question.

As an infrequent visitor to London (three, four times a year) it
was particularly noticeable to me how the numbers of homeless
youngsters in the capital had been growing throughout the
eighties. I had it in the back of my mind to write a novel on the
subject, and when the then Housing Minister, Sir George Young,
made his infamous remark that the homeless are the sort of
people one steps on when coming out of the opera,
I felt indignant enough to begin.

I wrote to the charities Alone in London and Centrepoint Soho
telling them of my intention and requesting information. Both
were most helpful, sending packs of material which proved
invaluable. However, it dawned on me eventually that if I was to
write convincingly about life on the street, I was going to have to
experience it at first hand.

Accordingly in the spring of 1992 I let my hair grow long,
refrained from bathing for a week or two and took myself off to
London and to Camden High Street, dressed in my oldest clothes
and dangling a bedroll. I spent three consecutive nights in the
area around the tube station, Pratt Street (where one of my
publishers had their offices) and the Lock Market. I was able to
strike up conversations with a number of homeless youngsters,
who thought I'd come from Bradford looking for work.

One night at one a.m. a man approached the doorway I was sitting in, deposited a bagful of hot Chinese food at my side and hurried off without a word. Another night I was hugged by a hulking Scots alcoholic whom I'd thought was about to murder me. Three nights – three warm spring nights were enough for me, and I was over fifty. What it must feel like at sixteen I shudder to imagine.

I ought to emphasise here that I don't claim, on the strength of those three nights, to have experienced homelessness.

A publisher friend had kindly made his lovely flat available to me so that I could sleep in the daytime, and I could have fled there at night too if I'd needed to. I was able to find out for myself what it feels like to lie on concrete for hours on end, to observe what goes on on Camden High Street at three in the morning, and learn at second hand about some of the dangers homeless youngsters face every night of their lives. This proved to be priceless when I was writing the book, but I don't delude myself that if I had to do it for real I'd be dead in a month.

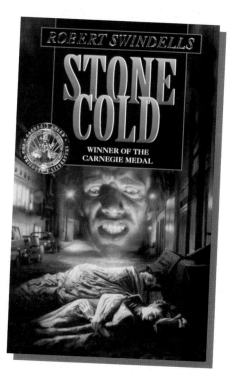

- Discuss in groups all the things you expect this novel to be about. What events might happen in it? Take your ideas from what the author says about the background to the story, and the book cover.

- Imagine that *you* are planning a story. It is based on homeless young people living on the streets of London. What ideas would you have for the **plot** (what happens in the story)?

CALL THAT A HOME?

- If you had the choice, which of these homes would you live in?
- Make a list of your top ten requirements in a home. You might include: heat, shelter, love, TV…

LONELY?

LOST?

AFRAID?

DIRTY?

SCROUNGERS?

COLD?

Imagine meeting these two people sleeping rough in the street.

Discuss with a partner the thoughts and feelings you would have about them.

Report back to the whole class.

LINK'S STORY

Now read the first page of the novel.

You can call me Link. It's not my name, but it's what I say when anybody asks, which isn't often. I'm invisible, see. One of the invisible people. Right now I'm sitting in a doorway watching the passers-by. They avoid looking at me. They're afraid I want something they've got, and they're right. Also, they don't want to think about me. They don't like reminding I exist. Me, and those like me. We're living proof that everything's not all right and we make the place untidy.

Hang about and I'll tell you the story of my fascinating life.

• Think carefully about this opening page. Discuss these questions:

1 Why has Link changed his name?

2 Who are the 'invisible people'?

3 Why are passers-by afraid of him?

4 What makes him say 'We're living proof that everything's not all right...'?

5 Why is Link sitting in a doorway?

• Now write some questions of your own. What do you want to find out as you read on?

STARTING YOUR OWN READING LOG

WHAT IS A READING LOG?

A reading log is a book in which you write down all your
thoughts, ideas and questions about the novel you are reading.

PROMPTS FOR WRITING

You can write anything you like in your log, but you might consider:

1 Setting – where and when the story takes place

2 Characters – the people in the story

3 Plot – what happens in the story

4 Language – how the story is written

5 Themes – ideas and messages you get from the story

6 Wide reading – how this story compares to others you have read

You could start your log with
the questions you've already
thought of, after reading the
first page of the novel.

This is how one student
began her log:

Monday 5/8/98

'Stone Cold'

*I've just started 'Stone Cold'. Page 1 is a bit puzzling. Why has Link
changed his name? Doesn't he like his real name? I think he might
want to forget his old life. Maybe he's one of the people on the front
cover. Maybe he's homeless, sleeping rough on the streets.*

*When I see beggars in Bristol I get a bit frightened. I normally
rush past them in a hurry. They're dirty and often drunk. I'd
hate to be like them. I reckon this is a story about being homeless...*

Now start your own reading log. Remember you can choose any
part of the novel to write about. Look out for these reminders
as you work on the unit.

LAST CHRISTMAS AT HOME...

Now look carefully at this section of the novel.

Christmas didn't help. I spent it at Carole's which was kind of her and Chris, but it was still the worst Christmas I'd ever had. For a start, there was my present. Carole and Mum had put their money together and got me this sleeping-bag. A really posh job. Quilted, waterproof, the lot. It must have cost a bomb and I knew they only meant to be kind, but it said something to me. It said they thought of me as a dosser – as someone who might always be a dosser, so he might as well be as comfy as possible. It hurt like hell, but I didn't let them see. And I've got to admit it's come in handy ever since.

Anyway, there was that, and then there was Boxing Day. Boxing Day Mum came round, and she brought Vince with her. I can only think that Carole had never told Chris the full story about him, or surely Chris wouldn't have had him in the house. Anyway, they came for dinner and stayed till one o'clock next morning, and of course everybody got drunk. Everybody except me. And once he got a skinful, Vince started making cracks about me. Don't ask me why. I was a disgrace, he said, stuffing myself with my sister's grub. Sitting there with my long hair and tatty clothes, making Mum feel guilty when she'd had nothing to feel guilty about. I was a scrounger, a sponger and a layabout, and I ought to be looking for work instead of sitting with a face as long as a fiddle, spoiling everybody's Christmas.

It didn't feel like peace on earth, I can tell you that. There wasn't a lot of goodwill toward men floating about. And the worst thing was, nobody stuck up for me. Not even my sister. It was then I knew I'd worn out my welcome, even here. So.

Here is an extract from the BBC TV script of the Christmas Day scene:

Carole: Come on, let's open your present.

(She picks up a huge parcel from under the christmas tree)

It's from me and Mum.

Vince: There's some of my money in there, and all.

Carole: And Vince.

(She holds out the present)

Go on.

Vince: Oh, he'll take it, he's good at that.

Lesley: Stop it, Vince.

(Link opens his present – it's an expensive looking sleeping bag. He looks around their faces – all smiling)

Link: It's brilliant, thanks.

- Work in a group of five. Each of you take the part of one of the characters:

  Link
  Lesley (his mum)
  Carole (his sister)
  Vince (his step-father)
  Chris (his brother-in-law)

- Think about Boxing Day. Act out what happens at the meal table. Use the account on p24 to help you.

- You could plan and write your play in the same way that the BBC **dramatised** the Christmas Day scene.

If you **dramatise** something, you take an existing story and turn it into a play. This happens a lot on TV. Can you think of any other dramatisations you have seen on TV?

WHO'S WHO?

Can you work out who's who?

- Ask your teacher for a photocopy of these pages, then cut out each picture and paste it in your log.

- Write a short description for each character.

- Study one character in detail and think of questions for all the others.

- As a class, or in a group of four, take it in turns to put each character in the 'hot seat' (see the Help Box opposite). Ask each character questions. Try to find out what kind of person each is:

1 What do they think?
2 What do they want?
3 What are they planning to do?

HOT-SEATING

You can hot-seat any of the characters in *Stone Cold*. You will need a volunteer to go into role as the character. The character is then put in the hot-seat.

The rest of the group asks the character questions. You need to find out as much as you can about the character.

COLLISION COURSE – PLOTTING MOVEMENTS

Read the section of novel from 'I trudged along Pentonville
Road' to '...be so unimportant that he'd vanish and no one
would care'. In this section Link meets Ginger. Ginger shows
Link around some of London's landmarks.

- Record in your reading log where Link and Ginger go.

- Record in your reading log where Shelter is. How does he
  get to Link and Ginger? How do you know this? Does it add
  excitement to the story?

LINK IN LONDON

On a photocopy of the map opposite,
plot Link's movements in green dots.

SHELTER IN LONDON

On your photocopy of the map, plot Shelter's
movements in red dots.

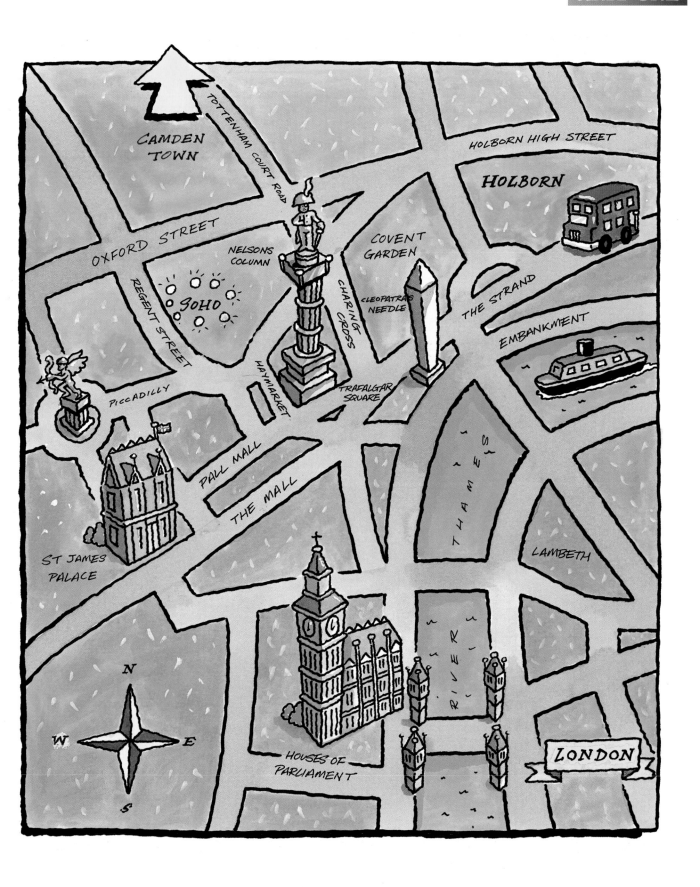

GAIL

Read on to the section which ends 'when something happened to jerk me back into the real world, it was spring.' If possible, watch Episode 2 of the BBC's dramatisation.

Very chatty, lonely?

Very attractive

She's got money

Heads straight for Link
– lucky chap!

- Draw a diagram like the one above. Write down all of your thoughts about Gail.

- Stick your diagram into your reading log.

LINK'S DIARY

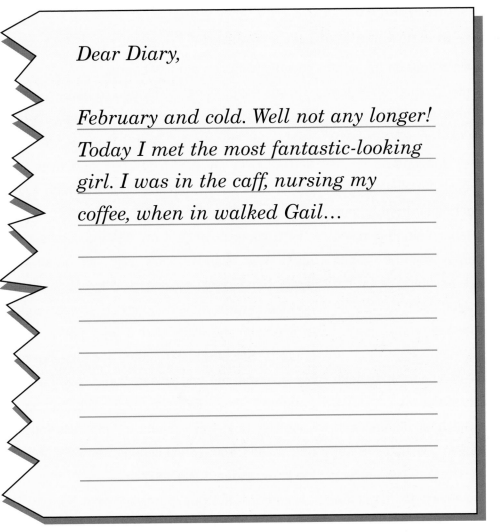

Dear Diary,

February and cold. Well not any longer!
Today I met the most fantastic-looking
girl. I was in the caff, nursing my
coffee, when in walked Gail...

- Imagine you are Link. Carry on the diary entry above.
- Think about how you feel. Think about the impression that Gail makes on you. Use some details straight from the novel.

HELP

Remember, you are writing to yourself in a diary. Be chatty and informal.

HORROR

Now read this passage from *Stone Cold*. Link finds out what
Shelter has been up to – and now his own life is in danger!

There was a short hallway with a door on the right and stairs at the end. The guy pushed open the door with his free hand and stood aside, holding the cat. 'Go on in, young man. I'll be with you in a jiffy.'

The room smelled of polish and was so tidy it looked like nobody used it. Heavy curtains covered the bay window. The only light came from a lamp which stood on a gleaming table. I stood dripping on the guy's immaculate carpet while he carried Sappho through to what I assumed was the kitchen. After a moment he called out, 'You couldn't fetch the dish, could you – the one on the step?'

'Sure.'

'You don't mind?' He chuckled. 'I sometimes think I'd forget my head if it were loose.'

I retrieved the dish with its little heap of mush and carried it through to the kitchen. He had the cat swaddled in a pink towel. 'Thanks.' He smiled. 'Thanks a lot. Just put it down anywhere. I'll get the coat in a minute.'

I went back into the other room, conscious of leaving wet footprints. If I'd entertained lingering suspicions on entering the house they'd now dissolved. The man was obviously a total wally with his cat and his obsessive tidiness. I couldn't help smiling to myself as I surveyed the room. Plumped cushions. Straight pictures. Gleaming surfaces. A place for everything and everything in its place. The occupant of this room was what my grandad used to call a Mary Ellen – the sort of man who wears frilly aprons around the house and may be seen in the garden, pegging out clothes. I was getting more complacent by the second till I saw my watch on the sideboard.

It was mine, all right. The one I'd handed over to the Scouser about a million years ago. I'd have known it anywhere. There was a tightening sensation in my chest as I stepped over for a closer look, and when the door slammed I cried out.

He'd come in without my hearing. Crossed the room. Was standing now with his broad back against the door, smiling a different smile. He nodded towards the sideboard. 'That was careless of me.' He chuckled, and it was not a wally's chuckle. 'Still, it doesn't matter does it – not now.' He looked at me and hissed, 'Link. Link the Stink. Laughing Boy Two, at last. Whassamatter, Laughing Boy – cat gotcha tongue?' He laughed and called towards the kitchen, 'Hey Sappho – got the kid's tongue, have you?'

I stared at the guy, paralysed with horror. We'd been right, Gail and Nick and me. This was our man. You only had to look in his eyes to know he was mad. He was totally out of his tree and he had me trapped, like Toya and Ginger and –

'Oh, yes.' He'd read my mind. 'He's here, the big Liverpudlian, along with the others, and a promising recruit he's turning out to be, too. Lots of potential. Bags and bags of swank. Would you like to see?'

'No!' It came out as a shriek. I pressed myself against the sideboard. 'I want to go home. Let me go.'

He laughed again, shaking his cropped sandy head. 'Oh no, lad. No going home. Not anymore.

You made me wait a long time, but you're in the Army now. The Camden Horizontals. Come and meet your comrades.'

'Let me go!' I knew it was no use, of course I did, but my brain had packed up. I didn't seem to be able to say anything else. He'd gone down on one knee and was lifting a corner of the carpet. I measured the distance to the window. If I could reach it – smash a pane, I thought –

'Here – have a gander.' He'd folded back the carpet and removed three or four short boards from the floor. 'I'll put the big light on so you can see better.' He got up. As he moved towards the switch by the door I made a dash for the window. The light came on. I grabbed for the drapes as he whirled with an oath, coming for me. I wrapped my arms round the curtains and swung on them. There was a creaking, splintering noise as the rail tore loose at one end and swathes of heavy fabric came down on both of us. Sobbing with terror I clawed myself free, slipped my pack and swung it at the window. The pane cracked but failed to shatter, and before I could take a second swing he was on me.

The strength of the insane. I'd come across that phrase, and now found what it meant. I'm not a small guy and he was a lot older but I couldn't break free. I bucked and writhed and lashed out with my feet, but he'd wrapped his arms round me and his grip was like bands of steel. My feet left the floor and he carried me across the room like he'd carried the cat, except he didn't croon or nuzzle, and when we reached the hole in the floor he threw me down and fell on me like a wrestler. I was pinned, lying on my stomach with my head overhanging the hole. A draught rose from the hole, carrying a cloying, sweetish smell. After a few seconds my eyes adjusted to the dimness and I saw them.

There were seven, laid out in a row like sardines. He'd done something to their heads – they were all like his – you couldn't tell if they were girls or boys – but I recognized Ginger by his clothes. His face was – well, I wouldn't have known him from that. I gagged, twisting my head to one side. 'Let me up!' I screamed. 'I'm gonna puke.'

He laughed. 'Puke away, soldier. You're the one'll lie in it, not me.'

With a partner:

- Act out this horrific scene in Shelter's living room
    - use the speech that is used in the novel
    - one person play Link, the other Shelter.
- Think carefully about how each character changes in this scene.
  Show these changes when you act.

Write about this episode in your log.
What makes it so scary?

SHELTER

Read to the end of the novel.

It was about 20.00 hours and I'd just begun my nightly patrol.

I marched along the Strand.

Laughing Boy One. That was the code name of the exercise. It was meticulously planned and beautifully executed, and now it's time for debriefing.

The killing, by a soldier, of the enemies of his country is not murder.

My tally of recruits stands at seven.

Tour

They've bags of swank, my lads. Shiny boots and nice short hair.

Check your equipment every time. Run through procedures. Know what's what. Don't fall into any traps.

Khaki

Confront the enemy, Shelter old lad. No retreat. No surrender.

Mission

Volunteers swell the ranks.

The enemy has attacked in strength and has been repulsed.

The Camden Horizontals...

Loners is what you look for in my line of business. Singletons.

...my chief function to kill, waste, do in – whatever you call it...

Get fell in, my lucky lads.

DAILY ROUTINE ORDERS 16
(PRISON LIFE)

- Look again at all these extracts from Shelter's Daily Routine Orders. Make a list of all the words and phrases that sound military.

- Imagine that Shelter is now in prison.

- Write some similar Routine Orders. Call your writing 'Shelter's Routine Orders 16 (prison life).'

- Use some of the words and phrases you have listed, and any others you can think of.

WRITING TO ARGUE

Read the following letter that was written to the editor of a local paper. It expresses a particular view about homeless people.

> *Dear Sir*
>
> *Last night I travelled into town to see a play. It was my wife's birthday and we had been looking forward to the treat for several weeks. The play was very good, but our evening was spoiled when we came out of the theatre to find several people sleeping in shop doorways and another two or three begging for money on the steps of the tube station. How can we call ourselves a civilised society if we allow these scroungers and layabouts to clutter up our streets? There should be a law banning such behaviour. I would like to see the police take a tough stance and move these people on, and then a pleasant evening's entertainment wouldn't be spoiled by such anti social behaviour.*
>
> *Yours sincerely…*

Write a reply to the paper, using your understanding of the issues and the experiences of homeless people from having read *Stone Cold*. You should aim to present an opposing point of view.

Plan your reply as follows:

- Make a list of the reasons the writer gives for being upset by encountering people sleeping rough and begging.

- What does the writer propose as a solution?

- List two or three reasons why his attitude is wrong.

- List three alternative solutions you can think of that will help the problem.

WRITING TO ADVISE

Gail is a journalist. Write a short article she submits to a magazine. In it you should aim to describe vividly the experience of homeless people in a large city, and also advise the Government on what needs to be done to help the problem.

Plan your article as follows:

- Plan an opening paragraph that sets the scene by describing what it is like to be sleeping rough on the streets. Use information and ideas for description from *Stone Cold.*

- Plan three paragraphs that advise the Government on three steps they might take which will help homeless people to get off the streets and begin to rebuild their lives.

- Plan a final paragraph in which you appeal to the public to be more tolerant and understanding of the plight of homeless people.

- Think up a really good eye-catching title for the article.

HELP

WRITING TO ADVISE

- Offer alternatives.

- Suggest ideas, don't tell the reader what to do.

- Get on the side of the reader – put yourself in their shoes.

- Use phrases such as:

  1 One reason why…   **2** A further difficulty experienced by…

  3 What can the government do? Firstly…   **4** Secondly…

  5 In order to help we all need to…

- Use **connectives** such as:

  1 Consequently   **2** Furthermore   **3** Finally

  to link up your ideas.

Newsroom

Look carefully at this picture of a newsroom.

Information can be beamed to the newsroom via satellite.

Journalists write their articles on word processors.

TV has pages of news which are updated. This is called Teletext and is like a TV newspaper.

Some stories need to be 'sniffed out' by reporters. Newspapers have reporters around the world.

Some stories can be found on the Internet.

Some stories come in on tape.

The editor decides which stories are used and where they go in the paper.

The sub-editor shortens stories to fit the space on the page.

The picture editor decides which picture is best and how to fit it on the page.

A photographer can go with a reporter to take photos of the events.

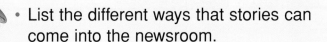

- List the different ways that stories can come into the newsroom.

- List the jobs that journalists are doing in the picture.

- Which do you think are the most important jobs?

A STORY BREAKS

A lot of news pours into a newsroom. Decisions have to be made –
which news story is important and which is less important?

Reporter Carrie Ferrant is about to watch the late film when she gets a call from her editor.

Carrie is sent to a fire at an old warehouse by the river.

Carrie goes to work finding out all the facts.

Can you tell me what you know?

It started in the basement. It's nearly under control. 5 men have been taken to hospital.

She then talks to some witnesses outside Red Lion Pub.

RED LION

We had to leave our house. We live too close to the warehouse..

We smelt the smoke about 1 o'clock.

Carrie phones in to the newsroom It is now 3.30 a.m.

Right. I've typed it in. You get home and get some sleep!

Fire swept through the warehouse of Swan and Sons in the early hours of this morning. Twelve fire engines fought the blaze, which could be seen 20 miles away..

In the morning meeting

The Warehouse Fire. Have we got an angle on it?

WHAT IS AN ANGLE?

An angle is a way of looking at a story. The story of the warehouse fire could be looked at from several angles:

- the bravery of the fire-fighters

- the loss of precious paintings in the warehouse

- the amazing survival of the church next door

- the possibility that the fire had been started on purpose (arson)

- burning chemicals seeping into a nearby river

- people living near the fire spending the night in a nearby school

WHAT IS YOUR ANGLE?

- If you were Carrie which angle would you choose?
- Which angles do these headlines fit?

FIRE THREATENS ART TREASURES

BRAVE FIREFIGHTERS BEAT WAREHOUSE BLAZE

CITY FIRE: WAS IT DELIBERATE?

- Now write the headlines for the other angles.

BUT WILL IT MAKE THE FRONT PAGE?

Top stories are printed on the front page. Look at the front pages of newspapers.

- What makes a front page story?
- Why are other stories on the inside pages?
- Why do some funny stories appear on the front page?
- Look at different papers. Do papers have different sorts of headlines? Why?

WHAT ELSE HAVE WE GOT?

WELL, THERE'S A PLANE CRASH IN INDIA - 100 DEAD.

A PLANE CRASH

36hrs

A MAN IN SURREY HAS BROKEN THE RECORD FOR NON-STOP BARKING- 36 HOURS.

THERE'S THE BIG WAREHOUSE FIRE IN LONDON.

BOMB ALERT

A BOMB EXPLODED OUTSIDE BUCKINGHAM PALACE. QUEEN WASN'T HURT, BUT A ROYAL CORGI WAS KILLED.

AND AN OLD LADY FRIGHTENED AWAY A BURGLAR BY TRYING TO KISS HIM.

THE EDITOR MAKES A CLEAR DECISION

NOT THE WAREHOUSE FIRE.

The editor chooses one serious story and one funny story to go on the front page. Which do you think he chooses?

LATER THAT DAY...

The morning edition of the newspaper has already been printed. But newspapers have later editions, to include news that happens later. Suddenly there is startling news from the warehouse. Part of the warehouse was used as a recording studio.

Now three bodies have been found in the smoking ruins. A famous band, The Sub-Zeroes, had been rehearsing in the building. No one has seen them since the fire.

ARE THE BODIES THOSE OF THE BAND?

Reporter Carrie Ferrant looks at her notebook. She talked to witnesses at the fire:

'Just before the fire I could hear music coming from the warehouse.' John Collins, 52, who had been drinking in the Red Lion opposite.

'We had a call at 11.43pm and responded as quickly as we could.' Arthur Morrison, firefighter.

'Thank God the church next door was untouched.' Alice Munro, whose flat overlooked the fire.

'We have no reason to believe anyone has been killed.' Jim Hardy, policeman.

'I did see some scruffy looking chaps in the pub. They looked a bit familiar, but I don't know much about pop groups! They went out together at about 10pm.' Landlady at the Red Lion.

'I couldn't hear anything from the warehouse at all. No. I can't remember if I was wearing my hearing aid, to be honest with you.' Sid Chesterman, 70, who lives near the warehouse.

CARRIE'S NOTES

Carrie made notes about the facts:

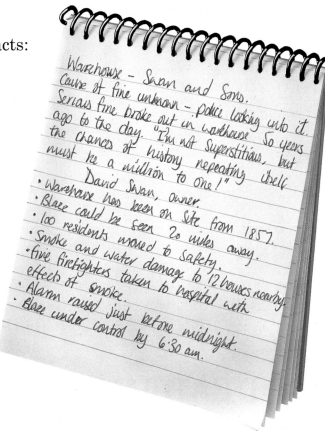

Warehouse – Swan and Sons.
Cause of fire unknown – police looking into it.
Serious fire broke out in warehouse 50 years
ago to the day. "I'm not superstitious, but
the chances of history repeating itself
must be a million to one!"
        David Swan, owner.
• Warehouse has been on site from 1857.
• Blaze could be seen 20 miles away.
• 100 residents moved to safety.
• Smoke and water damage to 12 houses nearby.
• Five firefighters taken to hospital with
effects of smoke.
• Alarm raised just before midnight.
• Blaze under control by 6:30 am.

Gathering your story

1 Decide on a new angle.

2 Read the statements and find bits that will fit the angle.

3 Read the facts on the pad and find out what is important and what fits the angle.

4 Write a headline and three short paragraphs to go in the evening newspaper, using the new angle.

HELP

NEWS ANGLE

- Always report the key facts – the story will be new to some readers.

- You can't use everything, so choose bits to fit your angle.

- Never lie.

- Pick out the relevant bit, using a highlighter or by underlining.

- Decide the gist of each paragraph.

- Think up links between each paragraph.

For example: *New information came to light when...*

A new lead has emerged in...

Evidence points to...

Some people think that...

Support for this view was given by...

Witnesses agree that...

Further proof came when...

HEADLINES

Here are some headlines that you could use for the evening edition, or you can make up your own.

THREE DEAD IN WAREHOUSE FIRE

MYSTERY DEATHS IN CITY FIRE

ROCK BAND IN FIRE TRAGEDY?

THREE BODIES FOUND IN GUTTED WAREHOUSE

ROCK LEGENDS DEAD?

ARSON ATTACK CLAIMS THREE LIVES

PICTURE POWER

A picture is worth a thousand words.

Choose the pictures that you think the following papers would use:

1 a pop magazine

2 a local paper

3 a national daily

LAYOUT

Look at this page from a newspaper. Match the arrows with the correct terms from the Help Box on page 49.

THE SENTINEL

NO. 10,181   2 SEPTEMBER 2002   50p

MP BACKS CUTS TO NHS BUDGET

D

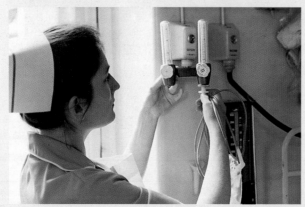

Plans Revealed

E

A ► Nurses are under increasing pressure

B ►

C

**Special Report
p6**

**Arts and Books
p10**

**TV and Radio
p30**

**Weather and Sport
p32**

HELP

Headline:

- The title of the story
- Large type
- Gives the most important fact of the story

Subheading:

- Under the headline
- Gives more information about the story
- Type is smaller than headline

Article:

- The story
- Printed in columns
- Small print

Column:

- Rows of print that run down the page

Caption:

- Line of print under the photograph
- Explains what is in the photograph

Design the front page of your own newspaper to show how the headline, pictures and story would appear.

PRESENTING THE NEWS

Could you be a newscaster? The job of a newscaster is:

- To introduce stories
- To write the story script so that most people will follow it and be interested in it
- To set the scene and give basic facts
- To lead into interviews
- To link different news items together

To be a newscaster you must:

- Explain things simply and clearly
- Use plain standard English
- Make good notes to read from
- Speak slowly, confidently and clearly
- Keep your script on the table, not in front of your face
- Make eye contact with the camera
- Glance at your notes but look up to the camera
- Practise a few times

HELP

Speaking standard English

- Standard English isn't 'posh', and it's nothing to do with accent.
- Standard English means keeping to words that don't exclude anyone, e.g. local dialect words that aren't used elsewhere.
- Standard English means using the standard verbs, e.g. *we were* rather than *we was.*
- Standard English means being accurate and polite, and slightly formal.
- Standard English means keeping up the slightly formal tone.

Try it

Read the news bulletins below. They are based on nursery rhymes. Try reading them as a newscaster.

- Can you keep a straight face?
- Can you keep up the tone?
- Can you read slowly and clearly?
- Can you make plenty of eye contact as you read?

Try writing and reading your own news bulletin about a different nursery rhyme, e.g. Three Blind Mice, Jack and Jill, The Old Woman who Lived in a Shoe.

Humpty Dumpty sat on a wall
Humpty Dumpty had a great fall
All the King's Horses and all the King's Men
Couldn't put Humpty together again.

HUMPTY IN DEATH PLUNGE

Humpty Dumpty fell from a 40 foot wall today. The King's Horses and Men who were in the area tried to put the badly injured egg-man Humpty back together, but could not. He was taken to Wallsend Hospital but doctors said he was dead on arrival. Was it a tragic accident – or did he fall, or worse, was he pushed?

Hey diddle, diddle
The cat and the fiddle
The cow jumped over the moon;
The little dog laughed to see such sport
And the dish ran away with the spoon.

COW IN ORBIT

Experts last night were trying to work out the biggest space mystery ever. How did a cow get into outer space? And when it reached the moon how did it jump over? Possible links are being made with the strange theft of a spoon back on Earth. Last night a corgi called Rex was helping police with their enquiries.

UNSCRAMBLING THE NEWS

The six news stories opposite have been chosen for a TV news programme for teenage viewers. They are in the wrong order – can you put them in the right order?

HELP

There are two types of news stories – hard and soft.

Hard news

- news stories that are just 'breaking'
- about important events

Soft news

- about less important events
- not urgent
- funny stories

Hard news goes before soft news. Can you see why?

- There is one soft news story among the six in the list. Which is it? Where would you place it?

- There are five hard news stories. The most important story will go first, the next most important second, and so on. Work out your own running order.

- If you had 20 minutes for the programme, how would you divide up the time? Work out the number of minutes you would give to each story.

1   A huge banner painted by thousands of children from all over the world has been put on show in Ireland. The banner is a mile and half long. It tells the sad story of Korky the Killer Whale. People who are fond of animals want Korky released back into the wild.

2   England footballer Stuart Pearce has resigned as manager of Nottingham Forest. The decision comes after Forest were relegated from the Premier League. However, Pearce has said he'll continue to play for the team.

3   Three bodies found after a fire in an old warehouse have led to tearful scenes. Fans of The Sub-Zeroes fear the bodies may be those of the band. The group used the warehouse as a studio. The cause of the fire is still not known. Police have asked anyone with information to come forward.

4   Going to the dentist is something people dread. But fillings could be a thing of the past thanks to a new invention – a tablet that you don't even have to swallow. But Dr David Ball says that people should continue to brush their teeth well. The drug is still being tested.

5   American pilot Linda Finch has reached Australia. She is following the path of Amelia Erhart, who disappeared 60 years ago when trying to fly round the world. Linda Finch is even flying the same kind of plane as Erhart.

6   The African children who have lost their mothers and fathers. Aid workers are working night and day to cope with children who are returning home to Rwanda. Three years ago thousands of families fled from their own country when war broke out. Around ten thousand children have no parents to go home to.

LINKS

Link sentences help news-readers to move from one story to the next. Here are some links from a news programme:

Hello, and first...

Finally...

Sports fans will be interested to hear that...

Next we move on to...

- Put each of these links before the story (on page 53) it leads into.
- Make up two more links to complete your bulletin.

DID YOU GET IT RIGHT?

Now look at the running order and times on page 60.

- Discuss anything which surprises you. Can you explain why the times are so different for each story?
- The news programme is aimed at your age group. How many of these stories would you expect to see on the adult news on the same day?

HIJACK! THE CASE OF THE MISSING BUS

You are a TV reporter and this is your big chance.

A school bus has gone missing on its way to summer camp in Scotland, close to where you live. It was last seen near Lago, a small town.

You call the Headteacher.

'John Grant here... What? Yes, that's our bus... How many?... 42 children and three staff... Where were they going?... They were going to Glebelands summer camp for a week... No, we've had no ransom demand. I can't believe there's a problem... It's probably just a silly mistake of some kind...'

GETTING THE FACTS

You interview local people.

They filled up with petrol about half past ten... Then they drove off... Yeah, the bus stopped and I think the brown van was in front. I couldn't see much from here. I thought maybe it was another teacher who had caught up with them for some reason.

We have no more information at this time. The bus was last seen at 10.32 this morning. Tyre tracks indicate that the bus came to a sudden halt, skidded, then moved off with another vehicle. We appeal for information from anyone who may have seen the bus, registration F745 CPH.

Some kids did come in. I clearly remember several had a coke. They were nice kids. I'm sorry if they have been kidnapped.

HELP

Interviews

It helps if:

- You ask open questions that bring out comments rather than just 'yes' or 'no'

- You follow up any hints in what they say

- You try to get at facts, because you can't just report opinions

- You try to draw out more information

Useful phrases:

Can you tell me more about...?

Tell me more...

Why do you say that?

List two further questions you could use to draw more information from the three witnesses on page 55.

- Now put together the information for your first report. It must take exactly one minute to read aloud.

- You can use some of these sentence openings or make up your own.

A school bus has...

It was reported missing after failing to turn up at...

It was last seen near...

Shortly before disappearing, the bus stopped...

Petrol pump attendant Joe Walker told us...

Tyre tracks in the road show that...

Headteacher Mr John Grant told us that...

In the bus were... from...

Police Chief Anderson, who is in charge of the case, appealed...

The bus registration is...

This is... reporting from...

- Record your report on tape or read it aloud to the class.

TWO HOURS LATER...

It is time for the next news bulletin.

What do we know about 'Free The Children?

Hmm... leader is a man called Jude Evans. Had a bad time at school, doesn't want other kids to have to put up with the same thing. He tried the same thing two years ago, but he gave himself up, and got two years in prison... came out last month.

This is a message from 'Free The Children'. We believe this country should be free from laws. We believe every person has the right to make up their own mind how they want to live their lives. We do not believe children should be forced to attend school. Schools are prisons. Children should be free to live their lives the way they want. The children of Sackville High have been liberated by us. We demand that this tape be played on radio stations throughout the country. Only when our demands are met will the children be released...

Well, I saw this big bus and this brown van in the wood. I couldn't see too well, but I think he had a red shirt. Yes, the guy in the red shirt stuck something to a tree. I don't know what. There was a woman too, in a big blue anorak, looked like she was with him. I didn't see any kids…

I know no more than you do. Everything possible is being done. We have a hundred officers on the case. We appeal to the kidnappers to return the children to their parents…

Will we broadcast their demands? I can't say. I'll speak toMrs Owens, who owns the station…

- You need to update your story. You can use some of these sentence openings or make up your own.

There has been an amazing new development…

It now seems that the bus was taken by…

'Free the Children' is run by…, who…

The kidnappers are demanding that…

Two years ago…

'Free the Children' believes…

Police say…

This is… reporting from…

- Record your new report on tape or read it aloud to the class.

SHOWDOWN!

- • Get into groups of three.

- • This is a timed activity. You have 15 minutes to get ready for your bulletin. Start timing yourself **now**.

- Look at the picture and make notes for your bulletin.

  1 What is happening?

  2 Where is the bus exactly?

  3 Why has it stopped?

  4 What are the police marksmen doing?

  5 What is the police chief saying? (You must make this up.)

  6 Who is driving the bus?

  7 What can you see in the bus?

- Decide who will read the bulletin and help them to rehearse.

- You might start:
  The Sackville School bus hijack is reaching a dramatic climax…

- Now record your third report.

- Listen to each group's report and say what was good about it.

AND NEXT...

What do you think will happen next in the story?

- Will the hijackers give in?
- Will they make demands?
- Will they make threats?
- Will they say why they are doing it?
- Will the police be allowed to help the teachers and children by bringing food and drink?

- Will any children be seen?
- Will there be talks?
- Will the second hijacker be seen?
- How will the atmosphere change?

- Use the questions above to help you to decide what happens next.
- Make notes on your ideas.

- Make up what people such as the police chief say. Add this to your notes.
- Use your notes to write a final bulletin.

How did we do?

Discuss how your group went about the task of working out what was happening and how to deal with it.

Were you sure of your facts?

- How did you decide what was fact and what was just a guess?
- How did you word the parts that were guesses?
- Suggest some sentence starters you can use to introduce information you can't be sure of. For example:

Some people are saying that...

Working together

- How did you deal with time pressure?
- How did you divide up the work?
- How did you decide who did what?

Original running order for 'Unscrambling the news'

Children separated from parents (six minutes)

Warehouse mystery deaths (three minutes)

Korky the Whale banner in Ireland (one minute)

Stuart Pearce resignation (two minutes)

Linda Finch round-the-world flight (four minutes)

Tooth decay report (four minutes)

Macbeth

AN INTRODUCTION TO THE MAIN THEMES OF THE PLAY

ROLE PLAY CARDS

In this unit you will study Shakespeare's play *Macbeth*. You will get to know the plot and think about why the characters behave as they do. You will also be introduced to Shakespeare's language.

Use these role play cards to explore some of the themes and issues you will come across in the play *Macbeth*. When you get your card, read through the notes and discuss them with your group. Then role play what is happening. It is better to improvise (make it up as you go along) so there is no need to write a script.

ROLE CARD A (GROUP OF 2)

Your character

You are very superstitious. You always read your horoscope. You have even been to a fortune teller.

What's happening

Your friend really wants you to go out to see a film. The film's called *Out of the Blue*. It is on for one night only. Your horoscope said to stay away from the colour blue all that day.

Act out your conversation.

ROLE CARD B (GROUP OF 4/5)

Your character

You like to be with your mates. You often meet up with them on a Saturday to go into town. Recently they've been talking about shop-lifting. You think some of your mates may have done this already.

What's happening

Your mates point out something in a shop. They dare you to shop-lift it. They tell you it's easy but you're not so sure. They try to persuade you.

Act out your conversation. Do you decide to do what they tell you, or not?

ROLE CARD C (GROUP OF 3)

Your character

Everyone at school has trendy new pencil cases. You're fed up with being the odd one out. You take some money from your mum's purse so you can have one too.

What's happening

You arrive home from school to find both your parents waiting for you and they are not pleased. You try to explain why you took the money.

Act out your conversation.

ROLE CARD D (GROUP OF 2)

Your character

You've been going out with your boy/girlfriend for some time but have always dreamt of being famous.

What's happening

You have just had a letter offering you a place at stage school. You are very keen, but it means moving away. Your boy/girlfriend doesn't want you to go. Act out the conversation in which your boy/girlfriend tries to make you stay.

Each role play card introduces a problem that can arise.

- Role play the situation and show the other groups what is happening.

- Invite the rest of the class to talk about what happened in your role play.

Did the characters do the right thing?

Are there any other solutions to the problem?

- What did you notice about how different people tried to **persuade** others to do something?

HOW AMBITIOUS ARE YOU?

AMBITION
To have an ambition means that there is something you really want to achieve.

AMBITIOUS
To be ambitious means that you really want to be successful.

With a partner:

- Choose three of your ambitions.

- Talk about what you would have to do to achieve these things.

- If you knew something about the future, how would it make you feel?

- Imagine a fortune teller has just told you that you will be a famous sports person. How would it make you feel? Would it change your life?

- Have a go at **predicting** some things which might happen to others in your class.

HELP

Predicting means being able to guess what might happen in the future.

...to travel the world

...to play for England

...to own an expensive car

...to rule a country

...to win the lottery

...to be famous

ACT 1 SCENE 1 – THE WITCHES

The opening of Shakespeare's play is very **dramatic.** Three witches open the play. They meet in a 'desolate place'. They arrange to meet Macbeth after a battle.

> **Dramatic** means 'sudden', 'striking' or 'impressive'. Here the opening of the play is designed to grab your attention.

A desolate place. Thunder and lightning.
Enter three WITCHES

FIRST WITCH	When shall we three meet again? In thunder, lightning, or in rain?
SECOND WITCH	When the hurly-burly's done, When the battle's lost, and won.
THIRD WITCH	That will be ere the set of sun.
FIRST WITCH	Where the place?
SECOND WITCH	Upon the heath.
THIRD WITCH	There to meet with Macbeth.
FIRST WITCH	I come, Graymalkin.
SECOND WITCH	Paddock calls.
THIRD WITCH	Anon.
ALL	Fair is foul, and foul is fair, Hover through the fog and filthy air.

Act 1, Scene 1

Work in groups of three:

- Read through the lines a few times.

- Try saying the lines in different ways:
  shout whisper speak quickly speak slowly.
  Listen carefully to the words. How do they sound?
  What differences do you notice about each way of saying them?

- Can you find evidence in what the witches say that:

1 They can predict the future

2 They might be plotting something

HELP

'Greymalkin' is the name of a cat. 'Paddock' is the name of a toad. 'I come, Greymalkin' and 'Paddock calls' suggests the witches have helpers who they can communicate with.

READING THE PLAY

The play is split into five parts. Each part is called an Act.

You are going to carry on looking at Act 1. Read the cartoon below.

THE KING HEARS OF THE BRAVERY OF MACBETH AND BANQUO, WHO HAVE WON THE BATTLE.

ON THEIR WAY TO MEET THE KING, MACBETH AND BANQUO ARE STOPPED BY THREE WITCHES WHO PREDICT THEIR FUTURES.

HAIL MACBETH, THANE OF GLAMIS!

ALL HAIL MACBETH THANE OF CAWDOR..

...THAT SHALT BE KING HEREAFTER

THEY ALSO TELL BANQUO THAT HIS CHILDREN WILL BE KINGS.

ROSS ARRIVES WITH NEWS THAT KING DUNCAN HAS MADE MACBETH 'THANE OF CAWDOR'.

TWO TRUTHS ARE TOLD...

IN ORDER FOR THE THIRD PREDICTION TO COME TRUE, MACBETH WOULD HAVE TO KILL KING DUNCAN.

MACBETH TELLS HIS WIFE ABOUT THE WITCHES IN A LETTER. SHE WORRIES THAT HER HUSBAND IS TOO DECENT TO CARRY OUT THE MURDER.

YET DO I FEAR THY NATURE, IT IS TOO FULL O' TH' MILK OF HUMAN KINDNESS.

THAT NIGHT KING DUNCAN ARRIVES AT MACBETH'S CASTLE, AND IS WELCOMED BY LADY MACBETH.

IF WE SHOULD FAIL ?

WE FAIL !

MACBETH TRIES TO PREPARE HIMSELF FOR THE MURDER. IT IS LADY MACBETH WHO FINALLY PERSUADES HIM TO GO AHEAD WITH IT.

- Try to watch a film of Act 1.
- Now read some of Act 1 as Shakespeare wrote it.

THE ART OF PERSUASION

Macbeth's castle, near the Great Hall. Music and torches. Enter a butler and many servants with dishes and service over the stage. Then enter MACBETH

MACBETH   If it were done when 'tis done, then 'twere well
It were done quickly; if th'assassination
Could trammel up the consequence, and catch
With his surcease, success; that but this blow
Might be the be-all and the end-all – here,
But here, upon this bank and shoal of time,
We'd jump the life to come. But in these cases,
We still have judgement here; that we but teach
Bloody instructions, which being taught, return
To plague th'inventor; this even-handed justice
Commends th'ingredients of our poisoned chalice
To our own lips. He's here in double trust:
First, as I am his kinsman and his subject,
Strong both against the deed; then, as his host,
Who should against his murderer shut the door,
Not bear the knife myself. Besides, this Duncan
Hath borne his faculties so meek, hath been
So clear in his great office, that his virtues
Will plead like angels, trumpet-tongu'd against
The deep damnation of his taking-off;
And pity, like a naked newborn babe
Striding the blast, or heaven's cherubin hors'd
Upon the sightless couriers of the air,
Shall blow the horrid deed in every eye,
That tears shall drown the wind. I have no spur
To prick the sides of my intent, but only
Vaulting ambition which o'erleaps itself
And falls on the other –

Act 1, Scene 7

In the scene you have just read, Macbeth speaks aloud his thoughts about the murder. He wants to be king, but he doubts whether he should kill King Duncan.

Below is a list of Macbeth's arguments. Next to the arguments are lines from Macbeth's speech.

I will be killed if caught	*I am ... his subject,* *Strong both against the deed*
I am a relative of the King	*Duncan* *Hath borne his faculties so meek, hath been* *So clear in his great office*
I am his subject and should be loyal to the King	*I have no spur* *To prick the sides of my intent, but only* *Vaulting ambition*
I am his host and I should protect my guest	*This even-handed justice* *Commends th'ingredients of our poisoned* * chalice* *To our own lips*
Duncan is a good King with good qualities	*I am ... his host,* *Who should against his murderer* *shut the door*
I will be damned in heaven	*I am his kinsman*
I am very ambitious	*his virtues* *Will plead like angels, trumpet-tongu'd against* *The deep damnation of his taking-off.*

- Match the lines in the play to the arguments.
- Which ones are for murder?
- Which ones are against murder?
- What do you think Macbeth will do?

Lady Macbeth is more determined at this point. She persuades her husband to go ahead with their plan to murder Duncan. Macbeth says 'We will proceed no further in this business.' But by the end of the scene he has changed his mind...

Look at the lines below. Translate them into modern English using grids like these. The first ones have been done for you.

Macbeth	Modern Meaning
We will proceed no further in this business	We will not carry out our plans to murder the King
I dare do all that become a man; Who dares do more is none	
If we should fail?	

Lady Macbeth	Modern Meaning
Was hope drunk? Art thou afeard?	Have you lost your nerve?
What beast was't, then, That made you break this enterprise to me?	
We fail! But screw your courage to the sticking-place, And we'll not fail.	

- Look at this conversation between Macbeth and Lady Macbeth. What are the details of their plan?

- How does Lady Macbeth persuade Macbeth to kill the King?

- Imagine you are directing the play. Explain to the actress playing the part of Lady Macbeth how she should persuade her husband. Write down five points you would make.

MACBETH	If we should fail?
LADY MACBETH	We fail!
	But screw your courage to the sticking-place,
	And we'll not fail. When Duncan is asleep –
	Whereto the rather shall his day's hard journey
	Soundly invite him – his two chamberlains
	Will I with wine and wassail so convince
	That memory, the warder of the brain,
	Shall be a fume, and the receipt of reason
	A limbeck only: when in swinish sleep
	Their drenched natures lie as in a death,
	What cannot you and I perform upon
	The unguarded Duncan? What not put upon
	His spongy officers, who shall bear the guilt
	Of our great quell?
MACBETH	Bring forth men-children only;
	For thy undaunted mettle should compose
	Nothing but males. Will it not be received,
	When we have mark'd with blood those sleepy two
	Of his own chamber and used their very daggers,
	That they have done't?
LADY MACBETH	Who dares receive it other,
	As we shall make our griefs and clamour roar
	Upon his death?
MACBETH	I am settled, and bend up
	Each corporal agent to this terrible feat.
	Away, and mock the time with fairest show:
	False face must hide what the false heart doth know.

Act 1, Scene 7

ACT 2

LADY MACBETH HAS TO RETURN THE DAGGERS TO THE SCENE OF THE MURDER.

MURDER

You have been called to investigate a crime – the murder of King Duncan.

- In groups draw up a list of suspects to be interviewed.

- Decide who will do the interviewing and who will be interviewed.

- Decide on the questions to be asked. (Remember to pretend you don't know who did it!)

- Use the table below to help you set the scene.

Who has been murdered?		
Who was in the castle at the time?		
Suspect	*Possible motives?*	*Evidence?*

In role play:

- Act out one or two of your interviews.
  Remember Lady Macbeth and Macbeth are lying.

Now write a police report of your investigation. Use the photocopiable sheet below.

Police investigation by _____

Crime _____

Suspect _____

Scene of the crime _____

Findings _____

_____

_____

_____

_____

_____

_____

_____

_____

Conclusion _____

_____

_____

Signature _____

ACT 3

A ghost plays an important part in Act 3, Scene 4. He has a
dramatic effect on Macbeth's behaviour.

MACBETH, NOW KING, INVITES BANQUO TO A BANQUET THAT EVENING. BANQUO IS SUSPICIOUS AND MACBETH FEARS HIM.

THOU HAST IT NOW, KING, CAWDOR, GLAMIS, ALL.

FAIL NOT OUR FEAST

UNKNOWN TO LADY MACBETH, MACBETH GIVES INSTRUCTIONS TO HAVE BANQUO AND HIS SON MURDERED.

BOTH OF YOU KNOW BANQUO WAS YOUR ENEMY

LADY MACBETH NOTICES HER HUSBAND'S TROUBLED MIND AND TRIES TO CALM HIM.

O, FULL OF SCORPIONS IS MY MIND, DEAR WIFE.

WHAT'S DONE IS DONE

BANQUO IS MURDERED, BUT HIS SON, FLEANCE, ESCAPES..

FLY, GOOD FLEANCE, FLY, FLY, FLY!

THE TABLE'S FULL!

AT THE BANQUET IN THE PALACE THAT NIGHT, MACBETH IS HAUNTED BY THE GHOST OF BANQUO, AND ALL THE GUESTS NOTICE HIS STRANGE BEHAVIOUR.

LADY MACBETH TRIES TO CALM HER HUSBAND AND EXCUSE HIS BEHAVIOUR. MACBETH SAYS HE WILL VISIT THE WITCHES AGAIN.

I WILL TOMORROW —TO THE WEIRD SISTERS

MY FRIENDS...

- Who is the ghost?
- Why is Macbeth so frightened of the ghost?
- How does Macbeth behave?
- If the ghost could speak, what do you think it would tell the guests?
- Complete the ghost's speech to the guests.

STAGING ACT 3, SCENE 4

A ghost plays an important part in Act 3, Scene 4. He has a dramatic effect on Macbeth's behaviour.

'The table's full!'

In this scene, Macbeth 'sees' the ghost of Banquo who he has just had murdered. But the others around the table cannot see what Macbeth sees.

Look closely at the following section of the scene:

ROSS: Pleas't your highness
                 To grace us with your royal company.
MACBETH: The table's full!
LENNOX: Here's a place reserv'd, sir.

MACBETH:	Where?
LENNOX:	Here, my good lord. What is't that moves your highness?
MACBETH:	Which of you have done this?
LORDS:	What, my good lord?
MACBETH:	Thou cans't not say I did it: never shake thy gory locks at me.
ROSS:	Gentlemen, rise; his highness is not well.
LADY MACBETH:	Sit, worthy friends: my lord is often thus,
	And hath been from his youth: pray you, keep seat;
	The fit is momentary; upon a thought
	He will again be well.

You are to **direct** this part of the scene. Work with a partner. Discuss the following:

• Directors of Macbeth sometimes use the actor playing Banquo in this scene, others just have an empty chair and space at the table. Which solution would you use and why?

• Think about how you would put this scene on the stage, and how you would direct the actors playing each part.

• Write a set of 'director's notes' to explain what you would do. Include details of what the actors should do (jump around, turn round, etc.) and how they should say their lines.

• If you are able, work with a group of other pupils playing these roles. Set the scene out as you wish it to be, remembering your decision about using an actor to play Banquo's ghost or not. Direct the scene, stopping the action to help actors get into their role. Help them to practise saying their lines in different ways.

• You should aim to direct a scene that shows Macbeth as a person who is becoming tormented by the murder of his best friend, and shows how the other lords and Macbeth's wife can't understand what is upsetting him so much.

• Compare the different versions: which works best and why?

HELP

Director's Notes

- Draw a sketch of how you would set out the stage and where different characters would be sitting.

- Photocopy the section of the scene from your copy of the play and write notes next to the lines to show what the actor should do and how they should say their line.

For example:

MACBETH: *Which of you have done this?*

Stares at the empty space, eyes popping,
then looks suddenly at everyone

Note of panic in his voice, shouting by the end of the line

A WITCH'S SPELL

In Act 4, Scene 1 the witches brew a spell. The spell is to show Macbeth the future. Their spell is made up of some *very* strange ingredients!

A desolate place near Forres. Thunder. Enter the three WITCHES

FIRST WITCH
Thrice the brindled cat hath mewed.

SECOND WITCH
Thrice and once the hedge-pig whined.

THIRD WITCH
Harpier cries, ''Tis time, 'tis time.'

FIRST WITCH
Round about the cauldron go;
In the poisoned entrails throw.
Toad, that under cold stone
Days and nights has thirty-one
Sweltered venom sleeping got,
Boil thou first i'th'charmed pot.

ALL
Double, double, toil and trouble;
Fire burn, and cauldron bubble.

SECOND WITCH
Fillet of a fenny snake,
In the cauldron boil and bake:
Eye of newt, and toe of frog,
Wool of bat, and tongue of dog,
Adder's fork, and blind-worm's sting,
Lizard's leg, and howlet's wing,
For a charm of powerful trouble,
Like a hell-broth, boil and bubble.

ALL
Double, double, toil and trouble,
Fire burn, and cauldron bubble.

THIRD WITCH
Scale of dragon, tooth of wolf,
Witches' mummy, maw and gulf
Of the ravined salt-sea shark,
Root of hemlock, digged i'th'dark;
Liver of blaspheming Jew,
Gall of goat, and slips of yew
Silvered in the moon's eclipse;
Nose of Turk, and Tartar's lips,
Finger of birth-strangled babe,
Ditch-delivered by a drab,
Make the gruel thick and slab.
Add thereto a tiger's chawdron
For th'ingredients of our cauldron.

ALL
Double, double, toil and trouble,
Fire burn, and cauldron bubble.

SECOND WITCH
Cool it with a baboon's blood,
Then the charm is firm and good.

Act 4, Scene 1

• Copy the cauldron below. Draw and label all the ingredients of the witch's spell. You may need to look up some of the words in a dictionary.

• Invent your own spell written in rhyming couplets.
  Try to write at least *eight* lines.

HELP

Rhyming couplets

Rhyming couplets are made when each pair of lines rhymes, for example:

Eye of newt, and toe of frog,

Wool of bat, and tongue of dog,

Adder's fork, and blind-worm's sting,

Lizard's leg, and howlet's wing,

Each pair of lines is called a **couplet** (from the word 'couple').

For your spell, you could use modern ingredients or think of different creatures.

Write a list of ingredients first. Then choose ones that rhyme.

ACT 4

The witches give Macbeth a glimpse of the future.
They also give him three more predictions.

Read the cartoon below, then discuss these questions in pairs:

1 How do you think Macbeth feels after hearing the three predictions?

2 Why do you think Macbeth decides to kill Macduff's family? After all, they are no threat to him.

3 How much has Macbeth changed since we first met him? He was described as 'brave Macbeth' at the start of the play. How would you describe him now?

ACT 5

OUT, DAMNED SPOT...

LADY MACBETH IS NOW SERIOUSLY DISTURBED BY ALL THAT HAS HAPPENED. SHE IS FOUND SLEEPWALKING, TRYING TO WASH IMAGINARY SPOTS OF BLOOD FROM HER HANDS.

A LARGE ARMY IS GATHERING NEARBY. MALCOLM GIVES ORDERS THAT EVERY SOLDIER MUST CUT DOWN A BRANCH SO MACBETH CANNOT TELL THEIR NUMBERS.

AT DUNSINANE CASTLE..

THE QUEEN, MY LORD, IS DEAD!

METHOUGHT THE WOOD BEGAN TO MOVE!

MACBETH IS TOLD THAT LADY MACBETH IS DEAD. HE STILL THINKS HE CANNOT BE CONQUERED, BUT IS THEN TOLD THAT BIRNAM WOOD IS MOVING

EVENTUALLY MACBETH AND MACDUFF FIGHT. MACBETH REALISES HIS MISTAKES WHEN MACDUFF TELLS HIM HE WAS BORN BY CAESAREAN.

MACDUFF KILLS MACBETH AND CUTS OFF HIS HEAD.

MALCOLM IS HAILED THE NEW KING OF SCOTLAND.

Ross has to tell Macduff what has happened to his family. He delays in telling him – why might that be? Think about how you would break some bad news to a friend.

- Write your own script of the conversation between Ross and Macduff.
- What do you think Ross would say to Macduff about the death of his wife and son?
- Now act out your script with a partner.
- Compare your script and how you acted it out with another pair.
- What were some of the differences?

PREDICTIONS

The witches predict the following things:

1 Macbeth will be Thane of Cawdor

2 Macbeth will become King

3 Macbeth should beware Macduff

4 Nobody 'of woman born shall harm Macbeth'

5 Macbeth will never be defeated until Burnham Wood comes to 'High Dunsinane Hill'.

- How have predictions 3, 4 and 5 become true?

- How does Macbeth react when he finds out that predictions 4 and 5 are true?

THE WOOD COMES TO DUNSINANE

Read this passage from Act 5.

Enter a Messenger.

MACB. Thou comest to use they tongue;
thy story quickly.

MESS. Gracious my lord,
I should report that which I say I saw,
But know not how to do it.

MACB. Well, say, sir.

MESS. As I did stand my watch upon the hill,
I look'd toward Birnam, and anon, methought,
The wood began to move.

MACB. Liar and slave!

MESS. Let me endure your wrath, if 't be not so:
Within this three mile may you see it coming;
I say, a moving grove.

MACB. If thou speak'st false,
Upon the next tree shalt thou hang alive,
Till famine cling thee: if thy speech be sooth,
I care not if thou dost for me as much.

I pull in resolution, and begin
To doubt the equivocation of the fiend
That lies like truth: 'Fear not, till Birnam wood
Do come to Dunsinane': and now a wood
Comes toward Dunsinane. Arm, arm, and out!
If this which he avouches does appear,
There is nor flying hence nor tarrying here.
I 'gin to be aweary of the sun,
And wish the estate o' the world were now undone.
Ring the alarum-bell! Blow, wind! come, wrack!
At least we'll die with harness on our back.

Act 5, Scene 5

How is Macbeth feeling here? Is he:
1 confident
2 brave
3 fearful?

MACBETH FIGHTS MACDUFF

They fight.

MACBETH   Thou losest labour:
As easy mayst thou the intrenchant air
With thy keen sword impress as make me bleed:
Let fall thy blade on vulnerable crests:
I bear a charmed life, which must not yield
To one of woman born.

MACDUFF   Despair thy charm;
And let the angel whom thou still hast served
Tell thee, Macduff was from his mother's womb
Untimely ripp'd.

MACBETH   Accursed be that tongue that tells me so,
For it hath cow'd my better part of man!
And be these juggling fiends no more believed,
That palter with us in a double sense;

That keep the word of promise to our ear,
And break it to our hope. I'll not fight with thee.

MACDUFF   Then yield thee, coward.

                                        Act 5, Scene 8

- Do you think Macbeth knows his luck has finally run out?
  Find the line where he seems to give up.

- Read on to line 34, 'And damn'd be him that first cries, "Hold, enough!".'
  Why doesn't Macbeth give in? Why does he decide to die fighting?

- What do you think of this decision? Do you admire him or not?

You have watched the whole play. You have worked on the activities in the first part of this unit. Use the 'Focus On Sheets' on the following pages to look at some of the characters more closely.

You could split into groups to look at different characters and then report back.

FOCUS ON MACBETH

Derek Jacobi as Macbeth, RSC, 1993

- What crimes does Macbeth commit during the play?
- Look at the list of words below which are used in the play to describe Macbeth (use a dictionary if you are not sure of their meanings). Which do you agree with? Which don't you agree with? Why?

brave	avaricious	wicked	mad
tyrant	false	devilish	hell hound
black	deceitful	fiend	coward
devil	malicious	monster	butcher

- How does the character of Macbeth change throughout the play? On a separate sheet, copy the graph below. Fill it in to show how Macbeth's fortunes and character change. Use some of the adjectives from the list above. It has been started for you:

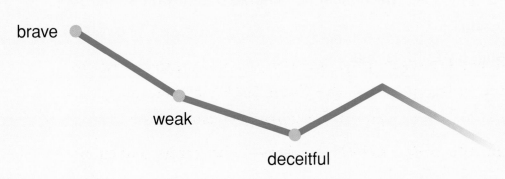

• Put the following events into order to show what happens to Macbeth.

1 Macbeth murders King Duncan.

2 He arranges the murder of Lady Macduff and her children.

3 He wins the battle and is honoured by King Duncan.

4 Macbeth prepares for battle. He is told the Queen is dead and Birnam Wood moves.

5 Macbeth is crowned King of Scotland.

6 He meets the three witches.

7 He arranges Banquo's murder.

8 He is beheaded by Macduff.

9 He revisits the three witches.

10 Macbeth fights Macduff and believes he cannot be harmed.

11 He sees Banquo's ghost.

• Match these lines from the play with the events above.

A For brave Macbeth – well he deserves that name

B I will tomorrow to the weird sisters

C Banquo, thy soul's flight, if it find Heaven, must find it out tonight

D The sovereignty will fall upon Macbeth

E Behold where stands th' usurper's cursed head

F All hail, Macbeth, that shalt be King hereafter

G I have done the deed

H Give to th' edge o' th' sword his wife, his babes

I I bear a charmed life which must not yield to one of woman born

J The table's full

K The Queen, my Lord, is dead

FOCUS ON LADY MACBETH

At the end of Act 2

Lady Macbeth persuades her husband, Macbeth, to carry out the murder of King Duncan.

- What sort of person is she?
- How would you describe her relationship with Macbeth?
- How does she react to the murder?

At the end of Act 3

- Which of the words below best describe Lady Macbeth?

  ambitious   persuasive

  in charge   brave

  ruthless   clever

- Can you think of any other words to describe Lady Macbeth?
- Can you find any extracts in the play which support your view of Lady Macbeth?

Cheryl Campbell as Lady Macbeth, RSC, 1993

At the end of Act 5

- Lady Macbeth is very influential in the play. Would Macbeth have carried out the murders without her?
- At the start she seems a strong character. Later she is tormented by what they have done. Put the following sentences in order to describe what happens to Lady Macbeth:

  1 Lady Macbeth sleepwalks and tries to wash imaginary blood from her hands.

  2 She plans to murder King Duncan.

  3 Lady Macbeth dies.

  4 She helps to make the King's servants look guilty.

  5 She tries to explain Macbeth's strange behaviour at the banquet.

- Now match these quotations to the events described above:

  A I'll gild the faces of the grooms withal

  B Pray you, keep seat. The fit is momentary

  C What, will these hands ne'er be clean?

  D He that's coming must be provided for

  E The Queen, my lord, is dead

- At the end of the play she is described as a 'fiend-like queen'. Do you think this is a fair description of Lady Macbeth?

FOCUS ON BANQUO

Banquo bravely fights alongside Macbeth at the beginning of the play. He is also with Macbeth when they meet the witches for the first time. He is told that his descendants will be Kings yet he is not tempted to do evil like Macbeth.

Christopher Ravenscroft as Banquo, RSC, 1993

- Which of these statements below might explain Banquo's behaviour?

1 He's content with what he has.

2 He's loyal to King Duncan.

3 He doesn't believe in witches.

4 He has no scheming wife to persuade him.

5 He is a good man who would never do wrong.

- Can you think of any other reasons?

- What sort of person do you think Banquo is? Can you find evidence in the play to suggest that he is:

    loyal

    brave

    honest?

- Banquo provides a contrast to Macbeth. Put in order the events that happen to Banquo.

1 He meets the three witches.

2 He is seen as a ghost by Macbeth.

3 He is welcomed by King Duncan after winning the battle.

4 He is suspicious of Macbeth's actions.

5 He is murdered but his son Fleance escapes.

- Now match these quotations with the events above:

A I fear thou playd'st most foully for 't

B O, treachery! Fly, good Fleance, fly, fly, fly!

C What are these, so withered and so wild in their attire?

D Noble Banquo, let me enfold thee and hold thee to my heart

E Thy bones are marrowless, thy blood is cold

FOCUS ON MACDUFF

Macduff is suspicious. He is worried about the way Macbeth is ruling Scotland. He goes to England to ask for help. He returns with an army to fight Macbeth.

Peter Guiness as Macduff, RSC, 1986

• Put in order the following events that happen to Macduff:

1 He kills Macbeth and cuts off his head.

2 He tells Macbeth he was born by caesarean.

3 The witches warn Macbeth to watch out for him.

4 He discovers King Duncan murdered at Macbeth's castle.

5 He goes to England to ask for help.

6 He is told that his wife and children have been murdered while he was in England.

• Now match these quotations to the events above:

A Thither Macduff is gone to pray the holy King upon his aid

B Ring the alarum bell! Murder and treason

C Behold where stands th' usurper's cursed head

D Beware Macduff. Beware the Thane of Fife

E Macduff was from his mother's womb untimely ripped

F What, all my pretty chickens and their dam at one fell swoop?

Writing about *Macbeth*

In this unit you have looked carefully at the play *Macbeth*. You have followed the plot. You have understood how Macbeth's ambition destroyed him in the end. You have used role play to help you think about the characters and what happens to them. Watching the play will have helped you to see how it all fits together. Choose one of the following three questions to use to write about the play:

1 What drives Macbeth to kill the King and keep on killing?

2 Do you think Macbeth is man or monster?

3 What is the most exciting part of the play?

HELP

Writing about the play

- You are asked for **your** views. Say what you think and back your views up with **evidence**. Find key lines in the play that you can use.

- Don't retell the story.

- Plan your writing into paragraphs. Each paragraph should be based on one key idea and at least one quotation as evidence.

- Start each paragraph with a topic sentence that expresses your main idea. Then give reasons and evidence from the text.

- Link your paragraphs by using phrases such as:

  'There are several reasons why I think...'

  'Firstly...'

  'Another reason is...'

  'Although some people argue that...'

  'Others think that...'

  'By the end of the play...'

  'In conclusion...'

Getting Ready For The National Tests

PREPARING FOR TESTS

The English tests at the end of Key Stage 3 test your reading and writing.

The reading test

You will be expected to read several pieces of text such as:

- A piece of fiction
- A poem
- Someone writing about their experiences, e.g. travel writing
- Someone writing about their opinions
- An information text

You have to show that you can:

- Understand what it's about
- Read between the lines
- Express a view about it
- Justify your views with evidence
- Explain how the writer made you think or feel as you did

The writing test

In the writing test you may be asked to write:

- A story or personal experience
- A letter or diary
- Information, such as a leaflet or guide
- An article
- A description
- A point of view

You have to show that you can:

- Adapt your writing for a special audience
- Fit your style to the purpose
- Choose an appropriate style for the task
- Express yourself in a clear and grown-up way
- Make your writing interesting and readable
- Spell and punctuate properly

ANSWERING READING QUESTIONS

Give yourself thinking time

Save yourself from mistakes by thinking first. Take time to:

1 Read the passage to get the gist.
2 Read the questions. Work out what they want.
   Find the key words in them.
3 Read the text again, with the questions in mind.
4 Underline, circle or highlight useful words to
   help you answer the questions.
5 Work out how much time you have and break up your time to get most
   marks. (The questions tend to get harder and carry more marks.)

HELP

Slow readers

Are you a slow reader?
Do you tend to run out of time in tests?

1 Save time by *scanning* the passage the first time you read it. Don't read every word – just enough to get the gist.

2 Read the questions carefully.

3 Read the passage properly the second time and look for the answers as you go.

HELP

Annotating the text

• Find words and phrases you can use in your answers.

• Choose the most telling quotations.

• When you spot something that will help with a question, write the number of the question next to it.

• Write words in the margin if you have ideas for your answer.

• You could use different codes for different questions, e.g. different colours for different questions.

Example

This is a passage about a boy called Barney who thinks he is being haunted. The question is:

What do you learn about Barney's family from the passage?

He was frightened, but only in a very tired way. If he got up and scrambled into bed with his sister Tabitha, she would ask him questions and talk all night. What he really wanted was to tell his stepmother and hear her voice, warm and cool at the same time, reassure him that there was nothing to worry about, as she went off to do something about it. But he dared not bother her. He knew that when mothers were expecting babies, they should have simple, happy lives and not be alarmed with ideas that their children were haunted or perhaps mad. And though his father was closer and kinder than he had been before he married Claire (in those days he always seemed to be going to work or coming home from it) he was still somebody Barney was not sure about, a jolly man who might turn out to be not very interested in his children in the long run. As it happened, Barney had only a few minutes to think about this, for suddenly he knew that sleep had crept up on him and taken him by surprise.

"I must be getting used to ghosts," he thought. "It shows you that you can get used to anything," and a moment later he sank thankfully into a kind of darkness without any dreams to trouble him.

Kind stepmother

Stepmother is pregnant

Own mother has died?

Stepmother – Claire

Father – rather distant, works

from *The Haunting* by Margaret Mahy

1 Find five things you would underline for the question: What is Barney's state of mind?

2 Find three clues to help you answer this question: Roughly how old is Barney, and how do you know?

3 Find four things to help you to answer this question: What have you discovered about Claire from reading the passage?

DIFFERENT TYPES OF QUESTION

You may be asked about:

- Characters and why they do what they do.
- The mood and how it is created.
- Things that are suggested but not stated.
- How the writer makes you feel towards the people, events or place.

You may be asked to comment on:

- The writer's choice of words.
- The way the text is organized.
- How it is told.
- About the choice of details.

HELP

Avoiding pitfalls

Examiners are agreed that the most common mistakes are:

- Retelling the story, and hoping the answer is obvious.
- Passing an opinion but not backing it up with evidence.
- Giving evidence but not explaining how it proves the point.
- Giving your answer but not showing your 'working out'.
- Talking about the characters as if they are real people, forgetting they are cleverly created by the writer.
- Over-simple answers, e.g. only giving one answer when you could have given several.

WRITING A GOOD ANSWER

Compare these answers to the question:

What have you discovered about Claire from reading the passage?

A

Claire is Barney's stepmother. She's a having a baby and Barney likes her. He doesn't want to worry her with his problems, especially as she is having a baby.

B

Claire is Barney's stepmother. Barney himself is quite young, and remembers the days before Claire came, so she has only recently married into his family. Her pregnancy suggests months rather than years.   Barney seems to trust her, as he wants to tell her about his problems, and he thinks of her as 'warm', someone who would 'do something about it' and 'reassure' him. Yet we are told 'he dared not bother her' and so he does not tell her about his problem. However, his desire to protect her from shocks suggests that he respects her. He has also noticed her influence in his father, who has become 'closer and kinder'.

- What is right about the first answer?
- What is wrong with the first answer?
- What is right about the second answer?

UNDERSTANDING THE QUESTION

The test paper sometimes gives you help in the form of bullet points.

Example

How does the writer create sympathy for Barney?

In your answer you should comment on:

- The way the writer describes Barney's fears and worries.
- The way the writer describes Barney's feelings for his stepmother Claire.
- The way the writer shows the reader Barney's thoughts in the last paragraph.

Refer to words and phrases in the passage to support your ideas.

- What is the actual question and how do you know?
- What is the purpose of the bullet points?
- Why is the last sentence important?
- Pick out the topics you are asked to write about.
- Pick out the clues about the way you should do this, or the approach you should take.

GIVING EVIDENCE

This is how to make good use of evidence:

1 Make a point

2 Provide evidence, a quotation if you can

3 Explain why that proves the point

4 Add any back-up evidence

5 Sum up

Example

What is Barney's reaction to the ghost?

Barney is unsettled by the ghost. He feels 'frightened' , and he'd like to tell his stepmother about it, so that she can 'reassure him'. He is not desperate, just worried 'in a very tired way'. The words the writer has chosen tell us that he feels fear but not panic. After all, he decides not to tell his sister or his parents, and he doesn't lose sleep over it. He is just apprehensive.

Point

Evidence

Explain

Back-up evidence

Sum up

HOW TO QUOTE

- Keep it short.
- Put quotation marks before and after.
- Choose the most telling words and details.
- Include it in a sentence if you can.
- Express your main point in two or three different ways.

Short quotations should be built into sentences instead of your own words, like this:

> He feels 'frightened', and he'd like to tell his stepmother about it, so that she can 'reassure him'.

Long quotations should appear separately, like this:

> Barney feels that the only person he really wants to speak to is his stepmother Claire:
>> 'What he really wanted was to tell Claire and hear her voice, warm and cool at the same time, reassure him.'
>> He feels that she is the only person he can really confide in.

HELP

Making the point

- How many times is the main point expressed in the example?
- You need to express your main point in two or three different ways.
- Think of useful synonyms to help you with this.

For example:

frightened
unsettled
apprehensive

NON-FICTION READING

Answering questions about factual texts is very similar to answering questions about stories, but there is more to say about:

- The choice of information.
- The order of information.
- The lay-out.

The examiner is still interested in:

- The choice of words.
- Telling details.
- Evidence, including quotation.
- Hearing how it proves the point.
- Points expressed fully and clearly.
- Seeing how the writer created the effect on the reader.

HELP

Remember what to do

- Read the passage.
- Read the questions.
- Read the passage looking for useful details to answer the questions.
- Annotate the passage.
- Plan your time to pick up marks.
- Make as many points as you can.
- Use evidence to support your points.
- Explain why your evidence proves the point.

PRACTICE

Work in a group of three to write an answer to this test question.

Read the following text.

Spend 30 minutes on your answer, including ten minutes' reading time.

This text is a pamphlet produced by the children's charity, *Save the Children*. It is written in the form of a letter and is designed to raise money to help suffering children in Africa.

The question:

Explain how the writer has tried to persuade the reader to donate money to the charity.

In your answer you should comment on:

- The way the writer describes the plight of the children.

- How the layout and organisation of the text contribute to its effectiveness.

- How far you think the writer has succeeded in persuading the reader to support the charity.

Refer to words and phrases from the passage to support your ideas.

URGENT

Because I know how much you care about children, I'm writing to tell you of our Appeal for the children of Ethiopia and Sudan.

The rains have failed, the harvests are devastated and food is running out fast.

That's why these children need your help now **more than ever**. *Our fieldworkers in Ethiopia and Sudan report that famine is imminent.*

But **it's not too late**. *By helping us now there's so much we can do for the children.*

A gift from you will get vital supplies of food and medicine to the children who need your help.

Save the Children can't make the rain fall. But together we can save thousands of young lives by acting **now**.

Thank you.
Nicholas Hinton, Director General.

ANSWERING WRITING QUESTIONS

Writing narrative

What people do well when they write stories:

- Openings
- Events
- Action

What people tend to forget:

- Paragraph breaks
- The importance of working towards the ending
- Keeping the reader curious about what will happen next
- What the characters are thinking and feeling.

Tips for top marks:

- Give insights into the mind of the characters and say what they are feeling
- Plan the ending
- Concentrate on telling words and details to create mood and character.

QUICK STORY PLANNING

Spend a few minutes on planning. Use this story sequence to help you:

1 Start the story	Get the story going. Set the scene. Introduce a character or two. Set the mood.
2 Introduce a problem	Make something happen that will upset the way things are – something interesting, so you want to see how people will deal with it.
3 Complicate matters	Make life harder for the characters, so they are in a fix.
4 Bring it to a crisis	Bring matters to a head – a clash, a crash, a row, an embarrassment, something that can't be ignored.
5 Make people adjust to it	Show how the characters react, or try to sort things out.
6 Resolve the problem	Bring the story to a fitting conclusion – perhaps reward the good and punish the bad. Settle matters.

Learn the six stages in order:
- Start
- Problem
- Complicate
- Crisis
- Adjust
- Resolve

(Some people learn **SPACE CAR** as a way of remembering. Use it if it works for you.)

Try planning this story. The first three stages have been
done. You plan the last three stages.

1	Start the story	New pupil starts school. We become friends. Lots in common.
2	Introduce a problem	But I notice he's the last into school, the first out and never there at lunch times or breaks. I ask him round to my house.
3	Complicate matters	He disappears altogether. A big search is started. His address is false. His phone number doesn't exist.
4	Bring it to a crisis	
5	Make people adjust to it	
6	Resolve the problem	

Here is another plan. This time the last two stages are done,
and you have to make up the first four.

1	Start the story	
2	Introduce a problem	
3	Complicate matters	
4	Bring it to a crisis	
5	Make people adjust to it	I realise that some of my friends are only interested in me for my looks, and that some people I never noticed before are actually quite nice. Jackie is one of these. I apologise to her, because now I know how she feels.
6	Resolve the problem	Next morning, I'm back to normal. But something has changed: I have new friends, and a better attitude.

Now use the grid to plan a story of your own.

Either:
  • A story about an unusual friendship.
Or:
  • My dog can talk!

QUICK PLANS FOR WRITING NON-NARRATIVE

Writing non-narrative is easier than writing stories because you don't have to invent a plot, and the style is often more direct. The thing that is difficult is deciding how to organise your material.

Use your planning time to do three things:

1 Group the ideas or information into clusters
2 Decide on the order
3 Create opening lines for each section

1 Group the ideas or information into clusters	**Should first aid or swimming to be put on the timetable in every secondary school?**
	Pros swimming Useful on holiday Reduces risk of drowning Healthy exercise Aids co-ordination **Pros first aid** Might save a life Useful in emergencies Needed for some jobs, e.g. nursing, driver — **Cons swimming** Something else would have to go Not all schools have a pool Time to dress/undress Problems with people forgetting kit **Cons first aid** Can learn this outside Cost of materials for practice Training staff to teach it
2 Decide on the order	1 Introduction – finding time for useful skills in packed curriculum 2 Pros swimming 3 Pros first aid — 4 Cons swimming 5 Cons first aid 6 Conclusion – swimming if we have to choose, but could fit both in a Life Skills course
3 Create opening lines for each section	School is meant to prepare pupils for life ahead, yet… It's hard to imagine a better case to be included in the curriculum than swimming… But there is another subject worthy of being taught to all pupils, and that is first aid…

Try planning for the following topic.
Either:
 • The state should pay wages for housework.
Or:
 • National law should be abolished in favour of international law.

The **very quick** method of planning non-narrative writing is just to plan the sentence starters.

TIPS FOR THE EXAMINATION

1 You know the mistakes you always make. Think of a way of remembering them and write it at the top of your examination paper in pencil. This will remind you to check.

2 Learn the spellings you know will come up, e.g. scene, rhythm, author.

3 Proofread. It helps to read your sentences in reverse order, last sentence first, then the one before that and so on.

4 Remember paragraphs when you:

- start a new topic
- move to a different time
- shift to a new place
- someone else starts to speak

5 Vary your sentences. Try the following:

- Begin your sentence with an adverb ending in –ly, e.g. _Warily, she looked round the corner._

- Embed a subordinate clause, e.g. _The man, who had been lurking in the shadows, sidled away._

- Begin with a preposition, e.g. _Through the door stormed the teacher._

- Use a short sentence. This is especially effective if it follows a number of long ones, e.g. _It stopped._

Can you suggest five ways in which this student's writing could be improved?

Mikey woke up and looked out of his window it was raining. He was late for school. He got up and got dressed. He didn't have time for breakfast. If he missed the bus again he would get another detention. When he got to school the bell had just gone great, Mikey thought. Then Mr Spencer came round the corner.

Black British Poetry

BLACK BRITISH POETRY: AN INTRODUCTION

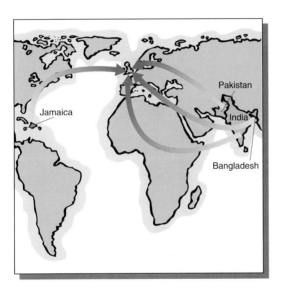

Throughout history people from all over the world have come to live in Britain. Recently many have come to work. Sometimes they were escaping from troubles in their country of birth.

The largest groups came from Caribbean islands such as Jamaica and from Bangladesh, Pakistan and India. In Britain there are now thriving communities from these and other countries. They are part of British culture.

When you move from one country to another you have to learn a new way of speaking, or even a whole new language. But no one likes to forget the way they speak. Poetry is one way of remembering. This is one reason why *Black British Poetry* has become so popular. Poets write down the rhythms and tones of their original language – often a form of English – for others to read and hear.

There are other reasons why so much *Black British Poetry* has been written. In this unit you will see how it is used to protest against racism. Also it is a way of celebrating the new voices that develop when minority groups have been based in Britain for many years and generations.

Before you read on, decide why it is important to study Black British Poetry. Read the statements below. Decide what mark you would give each one on the agree/disagree line underneath.

- It is important to read writers from a range of backgrounds.
- *Black British Poetry* can show what it is to be Black and British in a very powerful way.
- Black British people often have to fight for their rights and poetry is one good way of doing that.
- *Black British Poetry* gives the chance for voices to be heard that are often ignored.

Disagree   **Agree lots**

1   2   3   4   5

THREE POEMS BY GRACE NICHOLS

Tropical Death

The fat black woman want
a brilliant tropical death
not a cold sojourn
in some North Europe far/ forlorn

The fat black woman want
some heat/ hibiscus at her feet
blue sea dress
to wrap her neat

The fat black woman want
some bawl
no quiet tear jerk wiping
a polite hearse withdrawal

The fat black woman want
all her dead rights
first night
third night
nine night
all the sleepless droning
red-eyed wake nights

In the heart
of the mother's sweetbreast
In the shade
of the sun leaf's cool bless
In the bloom
of her people's bloodrest

the fat black woman want
a brilliant tropical death yes

The Fat Black Woman Goes Shopping

Shopping in London winter
is a real drag for the fat black woman
going from store to store
in search of accommodating clothes
and de weather so cold

Look at the frozen thin mannequins
fixing her with grin
and de pretty face salesgals
exchanging slimming glances
thinking she don't notice

Lord is aggravating

Nothing soft and bright and billowing
to flow like breezy sunlight
when she walking

The fat black woman curses in Swahili/ Yoruba
and nation language under her breathing
all this journeying and journeying

The fat black woman could only conclude
that when it come to fashion
the choice is lean

Nothing much beyond size 14

In these two poems, the fat black woman has moved from a hot, tropical country to cold London. She misses her home country and is not very happy.
Complete the following tasks, one poem at a time:

1 List any words or phrases that show the woman is not very happy.

2 Read the poem out loud. Say the words and phrases you have listed with real feeling and stress.

3 Draw two columns in your book. Label one *What the fat black woman likes* and the other *What the fat black woman does not like*. Fill in the columns with information from the poem.

4 Write a postcard from the fat black woman in London to a relative in Guyana (the poet Grace Nichols' country of birth). Include comments about each of the following: *the weather, people, shopping, general feelings, what she misses.*

Beauty

Beauty
is a fat black woman
walking the fields
pressing a breezed
hibiscus
to her cheek
while the sun lights up
her feet

Beauty
is a fat black woman
riding the waves
drifting in happy oblivion
while the sea turns back
to hug her shape

Poet, Grace Nichols

1 Sketch what you think the poet sees when writing this poem.

2 What is the shape of the poem? Look closely at how the lines are all a different length. Do you see a similarity between the shape of the poem and the shape of the fat black woman?

3 The shape of the poem and the sound of the words all create a *rhythm*. The *rhythm* is in both the poem and the woman. Write a poem that is shaped to show the rhythm of one or more of the following: ANGER, HAPPINESS, UGLINESS, SORROW.

Start your poem *Anger is* etc. Think about the length of each line and the shape of the whole poem.

You have read three poems by Grace Nichols. What do you think is the main *theme* of each poem? A *theme* is the main idea in a poem or a story, e.g. punishment, love, etc.

Work out how you would describe what her poems are like to a friend in less than a hundred words. Try to use the word *theme* in your answer.

DE GENERATION RAP

Dat guy BAD

He's *kicking,*

He's wicked,

CRUCIAL,

Cums round *here*

Wida smiley pon his face,

He CHILLS out,

Slides round,

Mekin circles,

He's safe.

Dis sista hard

She's *irie,*

MENTAL

Respect due,

She steps *cool*

Trods **easy,**

Hangs tuff,

Big up

An vitalistic.

When him pass thru

HARD VIBES,

Him wild,

Is a neat dude

SLICK geeza

A natural bro.

Made **up.**

She jus OOW,

Streetwise G,

She's **covered**

Fit Irie,

X.

People on de streets

Luv dem so much,

Dem **jus call** dem

DrrReadful*l.*

Poet, Benjamin Zephaniah

This poem uses *Black British* language to make poetry. It is the language of the young, the new generation living in Britain. Draw a table with three columns and label it as in the example below.

English language given a new meaning in the poem	English language words given a new spelling in the poem	Words that are new to the English language
bad	geeza	irie

- The poem is written in lots of different fonts. Each font looks like it should be read out loud in a different way. In groups, practise reading the poem out loud. Think of different ways to pronounce each word written in an unusual font.

- Choose your ten favourite words from the poem. Arrange them on a piece of paper or on a computer screen using different font types and sizes. See if you can add words to make them into a poem.

- You and your friends will use words and phrases that are not used by many other people, especially adults.

1 Write the words down.
2 Write a short sentence including each word or phrase.
3 Set the sentences out on a piece of paper or on a computer screen. Make them look like a poem. Add and knock out words to make them sound more like a poem. Experiment with font type and size. You might like to call the poem *My Generation*.

Checking Out Me History, by John Agard

Dem tell me
Dem tell me
Wha dem want to tell me

Bandage up me eye with me own history
Blind me to me own identity

Dem tell me bout 1066 and all dat
dem tell me bout Dick Whittington and he cat
But Toussaint L'Ouverture
no dem never tell me bout dat

Toussaint
a slave
with vision
lick back
Napoleon
battalion
and first Black
Republic born
Toussaint de thorn
of de Haitian Revolution

Dem tell me bout de man who discover de balloon
and de cow who jump over de moon
Dem tell me bout de dish run away with de spoon
but dem never tell me bout Nanny de maroon

Nanny
See-far woman
of mountain dream
fire-woman struggle
hopeful stream
to freedom river

Dem tell me bout Lord Nelson and Waterloo
but dem never tell me bout Shaka de great Zulu
Dem tell me bout Columbus and 1492
but what happen to de Caribs and de Arawaks too

Dem tell me bout Florence Nightingale and she lamp
and how Robin Hood used to camp
Dem tell me bout old King Cole was a merry ole soul
but dem never tell me bout Mary Seacole

From Jamaica
she travel far
to the Crimean War
she volunteer to go
and even when de British say no
she still brave the Russian snow
a healing star
among the wounded
a yellow sunrise
to the dying

Dem tell me
Dem tell me wha dem want to tell me
But now I checking out me own history
I carve out me identity

The British, by Benjamin Zephaniah

Serves 60 million

Take some Picts, Celts and Silures
And let them settle,
Then overrun them with Roman conquerors.

Remove the Romans after approximately four
hundred years
Add lots of Norman French to some
Angles, Saxons, Jutes and Vikings, then stir vigorously.

Mix some hot Chileans, cool Jamaicans, Dominicans,
Trinidadians and Bajans with some Ethiopians,
Chinese, Vietnamese and Sudanese.

Then take a blend of Somalians, Sri Lankans,
Nigerians
And Pakistanis,
Combine with some Guyanese
And turn up the heat.

Sprinkle some fresh Indians, Malaysians, Bosnians,
Iraqis and Bangladeshis together with some
Afghans, Spanish, Turkish, Kurdish, Japanese
And Palestinians
Then add to the melting pot.

Leave the ingredients to simmer.

As they mix and blend allow their languages to flourish
Binding them together with English.

Allow time to be cool.

Add some unity, understanding and respect for the
future
Serve with justice
And enjoy.

Note: All the ingredients are equally important.
Treating one ingredient better than another will leave a
bitter, unpleasant taste.

Warning: An unequal spread of justice will damage the
people and cause pain.

Give justice and equality to all.

Shaka, the Zulu Warrior

These poems are both about *identity*. *Checking Out Me History* is about the difference between what the poet is taught about in history lessons and what he wants to be taught. *The British* is a list of ingredients of all the people that together make the British people.

> • Read each poem several times. Try reading aloud in pairs. Talk about the differences you notice between each poem.
>
> • Compare and contrast the poems.

Five of the statements below apply to one poem, five to the other. Photocopy the statements and cut them out. Sort out which statement goes with which poem. Match the statements together in contrasting pairs.

This poem is written in Standard English as instructions for a recipe.
This poem is about what being British means for everyone living in Britain.
This poem is about one group of people.
This poem is written in a calm voice.
The theme of this poem is that people should learn about their own history.
This poem is about all groups of people.
The theme of this poem is that everyone should be treated equally.
This poem is angry about what history is taught in schools.
This poem is written how the poet speaks.
This poem is about what it means to be Black and live in Britain.

WRITING A COMPARE AND CONTRAST RESPONSE

Look at this list of connective words that show contrast:

however   whereas   although   whilst   but

Use these connectives to join your pairs of statements together. Order them and use them to write as a paragraph. Start the paragraph with a sentence of your own. You will need to make it clear which poem you are writing about. Try to include some examples from the poems to provide evidence of your points.

TESSA

Tessa   but stars
caress   speak wonders
the light   wonders
of the sun   foolish hands
kiss   that write foolish
the wind   letters
with the lips   will never
of a javelin   begin to understand
aim   that Britain is only an island
to the glint   surrounded by water
of stars   and for that matter
aim and sprint   an eye is an island
aim and sprint   surrounded by tears or smiles
for stars
know your name   and you chose to smile
stars understand   despite
the language   you chose to smile
of gold
and if silence   so run gal run yuh run
is golden   nah mek gold spoil ya
then stars   run gal run
are silence   run abreast of yuh vision

Draw a giant sun in the middle of a blank page. Write a large
letter S in the middle of the sun. Write around the sun all the
words in this poem that contain the /s/ phoneme (as in Tessa)
Your letters should *caress* the sun, like Tessa Sanderson's javelin.

Caress ——————— **S** ——————— Tessa

- What do you notice about the words you have selected?
- Think about the different ways of spelling the /s/ sound.
- Which words and phrases with this sound are repeated in the poem?

Now read the poem again.

HELP

By now you may have noticed that the poem has no punctuation.
As punctuation marks are signals to the reader telling you where
to pause, stop, and helping you to understand the sense, you will
need to decide these things for yourselves.

Rehearse reading aloud the poem with a partner or in a small group. Think
carefully about deciding which voices should read which words, lines or sections.

On a photocopy of the poem, make your own notes to help you to decide on how
to perform the poem aloud.

Practise until you are confident about how you are **interpreting** the poem.

When you have performed your reading, and heard others, discuss:
- What is this poem protesting against?
- What advice is given to Tessa Sanderson in this poem?
- What thoughts and feelings about Tessa Sanderson can you detect in the poem?

Rainbow, by John Agard

When you see
de rainbow
you know
God know
wha he doing –
one big smile
across the sky –
I tell you
God got style
the man got style

When you see
raincloud pass
and de rainbow
make a show
I tell you
Is God doing

Limbo
The man
Doing
Limbo
But sometimes
you know
when I see
de rainbow
so full of glow
& curving
like she bearing child
I does want to know
if God
ain't a woman

If that is so
the woman got style
man she got style

- What does this poem say God is doing when there is a rainbow in the sky?

- Why does the rainbow make the poet think that God might be a woman?

- This poem needs to be spoken out loud using lots of rhythm. Pick out five lines that you would say with lots of rhythm and stress.

- You should now be good at reading and performing poems with a distinctive voice aloud. Practise reading 'Rainbow' aloud. Read it with 'style'!

 Epilogue, by Grace Nichols

I have crossed an ocean
I have lost my tongue
From the root of the old one
a new one has sprung

- What is meant by 'tongue' in this poem?

- What is this poem saying in a very few words?

UNIT SIX

Scandal

NEXT DAY AT SCHOOL CHRIS AND RAHEELA HAND IN THEIR RESULTS

IN TWO MINDS...

Chris and Raheela have a problem. They want to accuse
David Watson of pollution. If they do he won't want to give
their school any computers.

Which is more important:

• to have a computer for everyone in the school?

• to have a clean river?

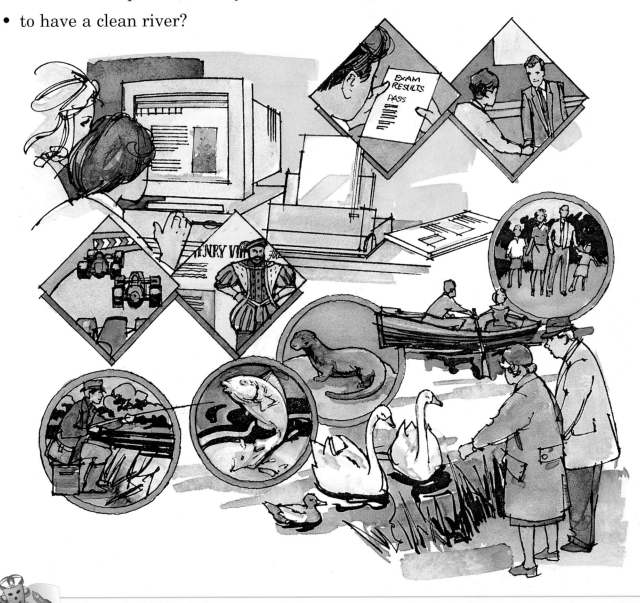

Look at the pictures above. Write down as many points
as you can for:

a) having a computer for everyone in the school

b) having a clean river.

GETTING YOUR MESSAGE ACROSS

Look at these two speeches:

A   Ladies and gentlemen, if the school has more computers we'll get better results and better jobs.

B   Can you imagine what a marvellous thing it will be for Redwood School, ladies and gentlemen, if every child in every class can have the use of their own computer? What happens at the moment? In every IT lesson we have to cram four pupils round one computer. As a result, three out of four students are bored. With one computer to one student everyone will be learning at a much faster rate. Our exam results are bound to improve.

Which speech makes the point best? Why?

HELP

Making a point

- Posing questions makes people think.
- Paint a picture of the good that will be done.
- Say exactly what you are asking for.
- Explain your thinking.
- Help people to see how they personally will benefit.
- Explain your point two or three times, to help it sink in.

Listening

In a group, remember some times when you have listened to someone else trying to persuade you. For example:

Someone asking a favour
A politician making a speech
A patient trying to make you see sense

- How did they get your attention?
- What tactics did they use to persuade you?
- What things put you off?

HELP

Appealing to listeners

A good speaker knows what people are listening for. For example:

- How will it benefit me?
- Is this something I *should* do?
- What will happen if I don't?

- How will it affect me, good or bad?
- Can I trust the speaker?

Persuaders also know that they can use:

- Flattery
- Bribery
- Threats
- Guilt

- Work in groups to plan two speeches:

Speech 1

1 Start planning the speech for a cleaner river like this:
  - *Ladies and gentlemen, think of all the advantages of a clean river.*
  - *Think of the anglers, who fish in the river...*

2 Think of two or three points to make about anglers, for example:
  - *fish will thrive in clean water*
  - *clean riverbank*
  - *will encourage more anglers*

3 Think of two or three points to make about the view.
  - *And what about people who just like a beautiful view...*

4 Think of two or three points to make about children.
  - *Then there are children who like to paddle or swim...*

Speech 2

1 Make up some sentence starters for Speech 2 in favour of more computers in school.

2 Under each sentence starter, think of two or three points to make.

- Choose which speech to make, and rehearse it.

- When all the groups have made their speeches, the class can vote on the best speech.

- In groups, discuss what makes a good speech.

Which speech makes the point best? Why?

THE TESTS SHOW THE SAME RESULT. THEY TRY TO CHECK THE SAMPLES THEY TOOK THE DAY BEFORE

DOES THE STORY STAND UP?

Chris and Raheela get their chance to
talk to the boss. But before they go in
they think hard:
What do they know that is **fact** –
something they **know** to be true?
What, on the other hand, is **opinion** –
something that **might** be true?

- Look at the statements below.

- Discuss each statement in pairs. Decide whether
each statement is fact or opinion.

- On a copy of this grid, tick the correct column.

Statement	Fact	Opinion
There are dead fish in the river.		
The pollution comes from the factory.		
Pollution is killing the fish.		
Stopping pollution is less important than a drug for old people.		
Stopping pollution is more important than a drug for old people.		
There have been cases of tummy upset.		
Clean water is more important than computers for the school.		

Chris and Raheela put their point of view to the radio station's boss and Mike, the legal expert.

- Split into groups of four. Choose who will take the parts of Raheela, Chris, the Radio Station Boss and Mike.
- Act out the discussion. Raheela and Chris must persuade Mike and the Radio Station Boss to report the story.

HELP

- Be polite and tactful.
- Be firm but don't be aggressive.
- Say what you want and why you want it.
- Tell them why you think they should help you.

THE NEXT DAY

I'LL TELL YOU WHAT WE'LL DO. WE'LL PUT AN ARTICLE IN THE SCHOOL MAGAZINE!

GREAT IDEA! BUT WE'D BETTER NOT GO OVER TOP.

I'LL TELL YOU WHAT. WE'LL BOTH WRITE ARTICLES. THEN WE'LL SEE WHICH ONE IS THE BEST.

HOW FAR CAN WE GO?

Chris and Raheela both write articles. Chris blames David Watson's factory for the pollution. Raheela is more careful. She describes the pollution as a mystery. She doesn't jump to any conclusions.

Extracts from the two articles are given on the next page. Can you tell who wrote each line?

- Using a photocopy of page 127, cut up the boxes.

- Put the lines under the right headline and in the right order.

- You do not have the parts of the articles which tell you about the factory owned by David Watson.

   1 What do you think Raheela's article would say about the factory?

   2 What would Chris's article say?

- Write an extra paragraph for each article, which fits in with the approach of the rest.

by Raheela Khan

Ten-year-old Darren Atkins was another sufferer, after taking a two-minute paddle.

A large number of dead fish have been found in the river. What has happened? It is a mystery.

Tests on river water prove that aluminium sulphate is the killer.

WATSON FACTORY POLLUTING RIVER

Other strange things have happened in the past few weeks.

Thousands of fish are dying in the river. They have been killed by poison. The poison is a chemical called aluminium sulphate.

We have heard that some people have had upset stomachs. They all live along the river.

MYSTERY OF DEAD FISH

An outbreak of upset stomachs is almost certainly linked to aluminium sulphate.

by Chris Bloom

Samples of the river water have been tested. They show very high levels of aluminium sulphate.

A ten-year-old boy, Darren Atkins, also came out in a rash after paddling in the river.

Several other incidents of pollution have been reported.

PANIC STATIONS

PEOPLE GET TO HEAR OF THE ARTICLE IN THE SCHOOL MAGAZINE. SUDDENLY PEOPLE COME FORWARD WITH MORE SYMPTOMS.

ALL THIS IS HARD FOR 13 YR OLD CLAIRE WATSON

FOR MONTHS SHE HAS LISTENED TO HER PARENTS ROWS

A PURIFICATION PLANT WOULD COST US £5 MILLION WE'D BE OUT OF BUSINESS!

WE'RE DOING ALL WE CAN!

BUT LOOK WHAT'S HAPPENING TO THE FISH!

WELL YOU AREN'T DOING ENOUGH!

THERE'S NO PROOF IT'S US!

THE REPORTER

MORE STOMACH UPSETS

CLAIRE, I REALLY DON'T WANT YOU GOING NEAR THE RIVER AT THE MOMENT.

THAT'S RIDICULOUS, CLAIRE. YOU CAN GO WHERE YOU LIKE!

AND IT'S ALL BECAUSE YOU WOULDN'T PAY FOR A PURIFICATION PLANT

BUT I'VE TOLD YOU! WE'D GO OUT OF BUSINESS!

CLAIRE'S DIARY

Claire, alone in her room, keeps a diary in which she records her thoughts. Whose side should she be on?

It is very difficult for Claire to make up her mind. She knows that the factory employs hundreds of people in the town. They would lose their jobs if the factory closed.

She knows that her father has worked hard all his life for the business. He is a kind man at heart and he cares about the town and its people. She knows that the factory makes pills to reduce the pain of rheumatism.

But she also knows that her father has failed to clean up the water because it would cost too much. She knows the problems the pollution has caused.

Here are two extracts from Claire's diary:

MAY	MAY
Monday 11th	**Tuesday 12th**
Another argument is going on. I'm in my bedroom but I can't help hearing. Mum's on at Dad again. They are talking about the purification plant. Dad says he can't afford it. I think she's right...	*Today Dad had a letter from an old lady. She told him how much his drug had helped her rheumatism. Suddenly I can't help seeing things differently...*

 Now go on and finish this diary entry.

Include all the reasons why Claire thinks her mother is right.

 Now go on and finish this diary entry.

Include all the reasons why Claire now thinks her father could be right.

SOLUTION

WHAT WOULD YOU DO?

Chris, Raheela and other characters in the story are faced
with many difficult decisions. They are not alone! Life is full
of difficult decisions.

- Six situations are described on the following pages. In each one a difficult
  decision must be made.

- In groups, read about each situation in turn and discuss:
- what you **could** do
- what you **should** do
- what you **would** do

CAN IT BE RIGHT TO STEAL?

John Brown's wife is suffering from
cancer. John hears about a wonderful
new drug. It is made by a big drug
company. It has taken the company 20
years to develop the drug. It has cost
them millions of pounds to make.

The price of the drug is £5000. John
does not have the money. He borrows
£2000 and offers it to the
company. He says his wife
will die if they do not
help.

The company refuses.
They say that if they sold
the drug cheaply to Mr
Brown, then other people would
want the same. If they did not charge
the full price they would lose money.

That night John breaks into the
company's offices. He steals the new
drug and gives it to his wife.

Was he right?

CAN YOU TAKE THE OFFER?

You are the Chairman of a Formula One car racing team. Your wife was a very heavy smoker. A year ago she died of lung cancer.

Your team has been sponsored by a soft drinks company. Last year your team lost many races, and the sponsor pulled out. The team is in a very difficult position. It was about to buy a new star driver. Now the team cannot afford him. At the last moment a new company offers to sponsor the team. But there is one problem. It is a tobacco company.

You are in two minds. Your team really needs the new deal. But your wife died from smoking. Do you accept the offer?

WOULD YOU GO ON TELEVISION?

You work for a company that sells burglar alarms. Many of your customers are old people. You know that many sales staff get old people to buy alarms by frightening them with stories of break-ins and muggings.

You are invited to appear on a programme which tells the truth about these sales. If you go on the programme and tell the truth, your friends at work will feel you are letting them down. You might also lose your job.

On the other hand, you feel that it is wrong to frighten old people into buying alarms. Do you agree to go on the programme?

DO YOU KEEP THE MONEY?

Your money has been taken by the school bully. Walking home you see something lying on the pavement. It is a wallet. Inside there is a pension book with a name and address on it. There is also £50.

You want to keep the money to buy a new computer game. At the same time, you recognise the name and address on the pension book. It is the grumpy old man who lives round the corner. Do you keep the money?

WOULD YOU TAKE THE COMPUTER AND RUN?

You go to a big store and buy a computer. You pay with a cheque. The assistant is very busy and makes a mistake. Instead of taking the cheque and giving you a receipt, he gives you your own cheque back and puts the receipt in the till.

Do you keep your cheque – or do you go back in and pay?

HOW CAN YOU HELP?

You go to a new school and are worried about being bullied. A tough girl called Kelly becomes your friend and looks after you.

Then another new girl called Sharon arrives in the class. Kelly starts to bully Sharon. Sharon comes to ask your advice. Should she report Kelly for bullying? You hate to see Sharon being bullied. But Kelly is your best friend because she looked after you when you were new. What advice do you give Sharon?

HOW AM I DOING?

Review your own progress as speaker and listener.

Make notes first. Then discuss them with two or three other people.

Seek and offer advice.

As a speaker

How am I different from the way I was two years ago?

When do I talk easily and well?

What holds me back?

What might help?

As a listener

When have I really listened?

What is it that gets me listening?

What prevents me from listening?

What might help?

As a member of a group

Which group situations bring out the best in me?

How would other people describe my groupwork?

Do I always behave in the same way in groups?

When doesn't it work?

What might help?

Drama

What have I learned from drama?

What kind of tasks do I respond to well?

When doesn't it work?

What might help?

Situation 1

CONTRIBUTING TO GROUPS

In a group, discuss:

- What are the other people thinking?
- Three good tips to improve the situation.

Situation 2

Situation 3

Situation 4

HELP

Running groups

Roles in the group are:

• Chair   • Scribe   • Spokesperson   • Notetaker   • Timekeeper

In Year 9, you should be able to take on all of these roles.

There is another kind of role too:

- The person who has ideas.

- The person who asks sensible questions.

- The person who brings you back to the job in hand.

- The person who is always thinking things through.

- The person who always looks at it from another point of view.

What other roles can you think of?

Which ones do you take?

All the roles are good roles. You need to be able to take them all.

Targets

Set yourself two personal targets for speaking and listening this term.

Choose something you need to improve. Keep it simple.

For example:

- I will speak in every group discussion.

- I'll offer to chair a group, and be spokesperson in another group.

- I won't butt in.

- I will show more interest in what other people say by asking questions.

- I will join a group with different people.

- I'll put my hand up at least once every lesson.

- I will take notes to help me listen for longer.

What the Dickens!

In this unit, you will read passages from one of England's most famous novelists, Charles Dickens.

Dickens spent much of his life in London but it was very different from the London we know today. It was overcrowded and noisy. Once, almost forty people were found to be living in a single room! There was disease. Many children died when they were very young. The city was full of thieves and prostitutes, and people lived in dreadful poverty. Criminals were treated harshly by the law. Prisons were terrible and Londoners still flocked to see public hangings.

However, London was a lively, bustling and colourful place with its markets and street entertainers.

Each evening, Dickens used to walk up to ten miles through the streets of London to get ideas for his writing. Many of his novels are set in and around London.

DICKENS' LONDON

In this passage from *Great Expectations*, Pip has just arrived in London. He goes for a walk.

So, I came into <u>Smithfield</u>; and the shameful place, being all asmear with filth and fat and blood and foam, seemed to stick to me. So, I rubbed it off with all possible speed by turning into a street where I saw the great black dome of St Paul's bulging at me from behind a grim stone building which a <u>bystander</u> said was Newgate Prison. Following the wall of the jail, I found the roadway covered with straw to deaden the noise of passing vehicles; and from this, and from the quantity of people standing about, smelling strongly of spirits and beer, I <u>inferred</u> that the trials were on.

- List four things about London which Pip finds unpleasant.

- Write a short description of a town or city you know well. This time try to make it sound attractive.

Here are some ways in which you could do this:

describe pleasant sights, sounds and smells

describe friendly people

describe attractive buildings

describe pleasant weather

> **GLOSSARY**
>
> Smithfield = the famous meat market
>
> bystander = passer-by
>
> inferred = guessed

DICKENS CAPTURES THE READER'S ATTENTION

Read the opening of *Great Expectations*. Pip, a small boy, is alone in a graveyard. He becomes afraid and begins to cry.

'Hold your noise!' cried a terrible voice, as a man started up from among the graves at the side of the church porch. 'Keep still, you little devil, or I'll cut your throat!'

A fearful man, all in coarse grey, with a great iron on his leg. A man with no hat, and with broken shoes, and with an old rag tied round his head. A man who had been soaked in water, and smothered in mud, and lamed by stones, and cut by flints, and stung by nettles, and torn by briars; who limped, and shivered, and glared and growled; and whose teeth chattered in his head as he seized me by the chin.

A good writer will try to capture the reader's attention at the beginning of a novel in order to make them want to read on. Often, the reader will want to know more and feel curious about what might happen next.

> • Write down five questions you would like to ask about this opening, for example:
> *Who is the man in the graveyard?*
>
> • In pairs, discuss what you think might happen next.

HELP

Try questions which begin with the words 'Who', 'What', 'When' and 'Where'. Don't forget to use question marks.

The man is an escaped convict and he wants Pip to help him.

- List three things the convict might want Pip to do for him.

- Suggest two ways in which he might make Pip do as he says.

Pip lives with his horrible sister and her husband since both his parents are dead.

- With a partner, act out the conversation Pip might have with his sister when he gets home from his terrifying meeting with the convict. You will have to decide whether he tells her what has happened. Think about the following points:

How do you think Pip felt?

What will he say to his sister?

Should he tell the truth?

- Write a short script of your conversation. Set your work out like this:

Pip's sister: *Where have you been?*

Pip: *Out.*

Pip's sister: *Out where?*

PEN PORTRAITS

Dickens was one of the best loved writers of his day. His imagination helped him to create characters for his stories which are so vivid, they seem almost real. Dickens spoke about his characters as if they were real, rather like you might discuss a character from *Eastenders* as if he or she were a real person.

Here are some of Dickens' most well-known and best-loved characters.

Smike
'an anxious and timid expression'
'patched and tattered'
'lame'
'dispirited and hopeless'
'could not have been less than eighteen or nineteen years old'
'round his neck was a tattered child's frill'
'timid, broken-spirited creature'
'shrunk back as if expecting a blow'

A character is a person in a story who seems like a real person but has been created by the writer.

Fagin
'very old and shrivelled'
'villainous and repulsive face'
'matted red hair'
'dressed in a greasy flannel gown'
'bright dark eyes'
'a threatening attitude'
'rubbed his hands with a chuckle'

Estella
'very pretty and seemed very proud'
'beautiful and self-possessed'
'as scornful of me as if she had been
one-and-twenty, and a queen'
'I found her irresistible'
'indescribable charm'
'her pretty brown hair spread out in
her two hands'
'She laughed contemptuously'

Mrs Squeers
'a large raw-boned figure'
'dressed in a ... night-jacket'
'with her hair in papers'
'a dirty night-cap ... yellow cotton handkerchief which tied it under her chin'
'presiding over an immense basin of brimstone and treacle'

Here are two more pen portraits. Use Dickens' words and your own ideas to sketch them.

The Artful Dodger

'one of the queerest-looking boys that Oliver had ever seen'

'snub-nosed'

'flat-browed'

'dirty'

'all the airs and manners of a man'

'bow-legs'

'little, sharp, ugly eyes'

'as ... swaggering a young gentleman as ever stood four feet six'

Uriah Heep

'a red-haired person'

'a youth of fifteen ... but looking much older'

'hardly any eyebrows, and no eyelashes'

'high-shouldered and bony'

'dressed in decent black'

'buttoned up to the throat'

'long, lank, skeleton hand'

NAMING NAMES

Dickens enjoyed creating names for his characters.

• Here are some of the names of characters in his novels. Read them to a partner.

Mr Bumble	Mr Boffin
Mr M'Choakumchild	Tiny Tim
Mr Squeers	Mr Gradgrind
Mr Guppy	Mr Murdstone
Mr Pickwick	Betsey Trotwood
Mr Podsnap	Mr Pecksniff

• Choose the three names you like best. For each one:

a) discuss what the character might look like

b) decide how the character might behave

c) draw a picture of the character

d) write a short description of your drawing of the character like those on pages 141 to 143.

DICKENS PAINTS A PICTURE

In *Great Expectations*, a young boy called Pip goes to visit an old lady called Miss Havisham. Pip has not met Miss Havisham before. He arrives at her house feeling rather nervous. This is what he sees...

 In an armchair, with an elbow resting on the table, and her head leaning on that hand, sat the strangest lady I have ever seen, or shall ever see.

She was dressed in rich materials – satins, and lace, and silks – all of white. Her shoes were white. She had a long white veil and bridal flowers in her hair, but her hair was white. Some bright jewels sparkled on her neck and on her hands, and some other jewels lay sparkling on the table. Dresses, less splendid than the dress she wore, and half-packed trunks, were scattered about. She had not quite finished dressing, for she had but one shoe on – the other was on the table near her hand – her veil was but half arranged, her watch and chain were not put on, and some lace for her bosom lay with those <u>trinkets</u>, and with her handkerchief, and gloves, and some flowers, and a prayer-book, all heaped about the <u>looking-glass</u>.

I saw that everything within my view which ought to be white, had been white long ago, and had lost its <u>lustre</u>, and was faded and yellow. I saw that the bride within the bridal dress had withered like the dress, and like the flowers, and had no brightness left but the brightness of her sunken eyes. I saw that the dress had been put upon the rounded figure of a young woman, and that the figure upon which it now hung loose, had shrunk to skin and bone.

GLOSSARY

trinkets =
small items of
jewellery

looking-glass =
mirror

lustre =
shine

• Write down five things you have learnt about the lady. For example:

She is wearing only one shoe.

• Draw a picture of the lady, taking care to include the details in the passage such as:

    – her white hair

    – her wedding dress

    – her veil

    – her jewellery

    – the flowers in her hair.

If you like, you could trace over the outline below and add the details.

The lady is Miss Havisham. She is an old lady.

Why do you think she is dressed like a bride?

Pip visits Miss Havisham again. On this visit, he is taken into another room. This is what he sees:

The daylight was completely <u>excluded</u>, and it had an airless smell. Smoke hung in the room, colder than the clearer air – like our own marsh mist. Certain wintry branches of candles on the high chimney-piece faintly lighted the chamber. It was <u>spacious</u>, and I dare say had once been handsome, but everything in it was covered with dust and mould, and dropping to pieces. The most <u>prominent</u> object was a long table with a tablecloth spread on it, as if a feast had been in preparation when the house and the clocks all stopped together. A centre-piece of some kind was in the middle of this cloth; it was heavily overhung with cobwebs and as I looked along the yellow expanse out of which I remember its seeming to grow like a black fungus, I saw speckled-legged spiders with blotchy bodies running home to it, and running out from it.

I heard the mice too, rattling behind the panels. The black-beetles took no notice and groped about the <u>hearth</u> in a <u>ponderous</u> elderly way, as if they were short-sighted and hard of hearing, and not on terms with one another. These crawling things had fascinated my attention and I was watching them from a distance, when Miss Havisham laid a hand upon my shoulder. In her other hand she had a crutch-headed stick on which she leaned, and she looked like the Witch of the place.

'This,' said she, pointing to the long table with her stick, 'is where I will be laid when I am dead. They shall come and look at me here.'

With some vague <u>misgiving</u> that she might get upon the table then and there and die at once, I shrank under her touch.

'What do you think that is?' she asked me, again pointing with her stick; 'that, where those cobwebs are?'

'I can't guess what it is, ma'am.'

'It's a great cake. A bride-cake. Mine!'

GLOSSARY

excluded = shut out   hearth = fireplace

spacious = large   ponderous = heavy

prominent = obvious   misgiving = fear

Make a list of six things you can find in the above picture which are described in the passage. Use the exact words from the passage, like this:

speckled-legged spiders with blotchy bodies

When Miss Havisham was a young woman, she was going to be married.
The man she was going to marry jilted her. This means that he decided not to marry her just before the wedding.
This broke her heart and she never recovered. Everything in the room has been left just as it was all those years ago.

Dickens has painted very clear pictures of Miss Havisham and the room. One way in which he has helped us to imagine the scene is by using **adjectives**.

An adjective is a word which describes something, for example:

bright jewels

young woman

blotchy bodies

long table

Look through either the description of Miss Havisham on page 145 or the description of the room on page 147. Find ten adjectives which describe things clearly.

• Describe three people using one telling detail that really gives a sudden sharp impression.

• Write a long paragraph describing a person or a place.

• Share your description with a partner. Pick out the three best words or details used.

HELP

Descriptive detail

Clever writers use one or two telling details instead of a full explanation. The details give you a sudden sharp impression.

A good example is the way many writers describe a person's face by telling you about just one feature, for example:

He had cruel eyes.
Her mouth was a red gash.
She had plump strawberry lips.

Writers also choose surprising adjectives, for example:

Blotchy bodies
Bright jewels
Speckle-legged spiders

Dickens only tells us one thing about Miss Haversham's face: the brightness of her sunken eyes.

GOOSEBUMPS

Pip is frightened by what he has seen at Miss Havisham's house. Later, in the garden, he thinks he sees something:

It was in this place, and at this moment, that a strange thing happened. I thought it a strange thing then, and I thought it a stranger thing long afterwards. I turned my eyes – a little dimmed by looking up at the frosty light – towards a great wooden beam in a low <u>nook</u> of the building near me on my right hand, and I saw a figure hanging there by the neck. A figure all in yellow white, with but one shoe to the feet; and it hung so, that I could see that the faded <u>trimmings</u> of the dress were like earthy paper, and that the face was Miss Havisham's, with a movement going over the whole <u>countenance</u> as if she were trying to call me. In the terror of seeing the figure, and in the terror of being certain that it had not been there a moment before, I at first ran from it, and then ran towards it. And my terror was greatest of all, when I found no figure there.

GLOSSARY

nook = corner

trimmings = decoration

countenance = face

- What did Pip see?
- Find two details which make the vision especially horrible.
- Find words that are repeated to emphasise how scary it was.

A Christmas Carol is another story by Dickens. In *A Christmas Carol*, Ebenezer Scrooge is a miser. He hates spending money and he doesn't like people to enjoy themselves. One Christmas, he is visited by four ghosts. The ghosts teach Scrooge that he should be more kind and more generous. Read these descriptions of three of the ghosts:

It was a strange figure – like a child; yet not so like a child as like an old man. Its hair, which hung about its head and down its back, was white, as if with age; and yet the face had not a wrinkle in it, and the tenderest <u>bloom</u> was on the skin. The arms were very long and muscular; the hands the same, as if its hold were of uncommon strength. Its legs and feet, most delicately formed, were bare. It wore a tunic of the purest white; and round its waist was bound a <u>lustrous</u> belt, the <u>sheen</u> of which was beautiful. It held a branch of fresh green holly in its hand; and had its dress <u>trimmed</u> with summer flowers. But the strangest thing about it was, that from the crown of its head there sprang a bright clear jet of light.

It was clothed in one simple deep green robe bordered with white fur. This garment hung so loosely on the figure, that its breast was bare. Its feet, beneath the folds of the garment, were also bare; and on its head it wore no other covering than a holly wreath, set here and there with shining icicles. Its dark-brown curls were long and free; free as its <u>genial</u> face, its sparkling eye, its open hand, its cheery voice and its joyful air. Round its middle was an antique <u>scabbard</u>; but no sword was in it, and the ancient sheath was eaten up with rust.

The Phantom slowly, gravely, silently approached. It was <u>shrouded</u> in a deep black garment, which <u>concealed</u> its head, its face, its form, and left nothing of it visible, save one outstretched hand. But for this, it would have been difficult to detach its figure from the night, and separate it from the darkness by which it was surrounded. The Spirit neither spoke nor moved.

GLOSSARY

bloom = rosy pink colour

lustrous = shiny

sheen = brightness

trimmed = decorated

genial = friendly

scabbard = a case for the sword

shrouded = wrapped like a dead body

concealed = hidden

Look at the illustrations of the three ghosts.
Match each illustration to the description.

Find three words or groups of words from each description on page 151 that helped you to match it to the illustration.

- Think about how the ghosts are described.

1. Which is the most friendly? Give two reasons for your answer.

2. Which ghost sounds the most strange? Give two reasons for your answer.

3. Which ghost sounds the most frightening? Give two reasons for your answer.

Oliver Twist is a story Dickens wrote about cruelty to children. In *Oliver Twist*, the orphan Oliver is sent to live in a workhouse.

George Cruikshank

• Read the following passage. Oliver is made to ask the master for more food.

• Think about how Oliver felt and what the master might do.

The room in which the boys were fed was a large hall, with a <u>copper</u> at one end, out of which the master, dressed in an apron for the purpose, and assisted by one or two women, ladled the <u>gruel</u> at meal-times. The bowls never wanted washing. The boys polished them with their spoons till they shone again. Oliver Twist and his companions suffered the tortures of slow starvation for three months: at last they got so wild with hunger, that one boy, who was tall for his age, and hadn't been used to that sort of thing (for his father had kept a small cookshop), hinted darkly to his companions, that unless he had another basin of gruel, he was afraid he might some night happen to eat the boy who slept next him, who happened to be a weakly youth of tender age. He had a wild, hungry eye; and they believed him. A <u>council</u> was held; <u>lots were cast</u> who should walk up to the master after supper that evening, and ask for more; and it fell to Oliver Twist.

The evening arrived; the boys took their places. The master, in his cook's uniform, <u>stationed himself</u> at the copper; his assistants ranged themselves behind him; the gruel was served out; and a long <u>grace</u> was said. The gruel disappeared; the boys whispered to each other, and winked at Oliver, while his next neighbours nudged him. Child as he was, he was desperate with hunger, and reckless with misery. He rose from the table, and advancing to the master, basin and spoon in hand, said:

'Please, sir, I want some more.'

GLOSSARY

copper = large pot

gruel = thin porridge

council = meeting

lots were cast = had a draw to decide something

stationed himself = stood

grace = prayer said before a meal

SO WHAT'S NEW?

Dickens wrote *Oliver Twist* in 1837. Here are two more novelists talking about boys. One is writing nearly 70 years later, and the other is writing about 150 years later.

From 1913:

William remained a year at his new post in Nottingham. He was studying hard, and growing serious. Something seemed to be fretting him. Still he went out to the dances and the river parties. He came home very late at night, and sat yet longer studying. His mother implored him to take more care, to do one thing or another.
'Dance if you want to dance, my son; but don't think you can work in an office and then amuse yourself, and then study on top of it all. You can't; the human frame won't stand it. Do one thing or the other – amuse yourself or learn Latin; but don't try to do both'.

From *Sons and Lovers* by D.H. Lawrence

From 1992:

Simon Martin sprawled over the three chairs outside the staffroom door. He'd been sent there for being a nuisance in Assembly. He'd only arrived four minutes earlier, and already he was bored halfway out of his skull. He'd tried whistling (and been told off for it by Miss Arnott on her way in). He'd even tried seeing how many different clicking noises he could make with his tongue (and been told off for it by Mr Spencer as he walked past.)

From *Flour Babies* by Anne Fine

Compare the passages from *Oliver Twist, Sons and Lovers* and *Flour Babies,* and explain what changes you can see over time.

HELP

Comparisons

Look for changes in

- The content, e.g. behaviour, lifestyle
- The language and style, e.g. vocabulary, expression
- The tone or approach, e.g. how formal it is, the voice of the narrator

It helps to organise your thoughts if you make a grid with the three features down the left hand side, and the names of the novels across the top.

Read the passage from *Oliver Twist* again.

- Find five things that are typical of Dickens' writing.
- Describe Dickens' style of writing.
- How does Dickens make you sympathise with Oliver?

HELP

Perspective

Perspective is viewpoint. It's where we stand as we follow the events of the story. For example, Dickens makes us see the events through Oliver's eyes. He does this by:

- Telling us how Oliver is feeling
- Telling us what Oliver is thinking
- Telling us what Oliver sees and does
- Describing Oliver's suffering
- Not telling us much about the other characters
- Using words which influence our reactions, e.g. 'reckless with misery'

What do you think might happen to Oliver as a result of him asking for more?

Choose one of the following:

a) He is given some more food

b) He is beaten

c) He is thrown out of the workhouse

d) He gets a telling off

- In pairs, act out the scene four times trying these different reactions.

- Write a short passage (about 12 to 15 lines) which continues the story of Oliver after he has asked for more.

HELP

Writing in the style of Dickens

- Read aloud the passage from *Oliver Twist* to get the feel of the language

- Borrow one of his long sentences and use your own words in it

- Think like a Victorian, write 'in role'

- Use the same kind of grand words

- Borrow some of the words Dickens uses

- Keep up the big, confident voice of someone telling a story

- Include several descriptive details instead of 'big picture' statements

Although Dickens wrote about very serious things he wrote about them in an amusing way. His writing would make people laugh.

Now read what happens next in the story of *Oliver Twist*.

The master was a fat, healthy man; but he turned very pale.
He gazed in stupefied astonishment on the small rebel for
some seconds, and then clung for support to the copper.
The assistants were paralysed with wonder; the boys with fear.
'What?' said the master at length, in a faint voice.
'Please, sir,' replied Oliver, 'I want some more.'

- Write down three amusing things about the way the master and his assistants are described.

A GRISLY END

Not all of Dickens' writing is humorous though. Later on in the story *Oliver Twist*, Oliver joins a gang of pickpockets. Among the people he meets is a burglar called Bill Sikes, and Bill's girlfriend Nancy. Nancy knows that Bill is bad and she goes behind his back to help Oliver. Bill finds out. Nancy begs for mercy, but he murders her.

The housebreaker freed one arm, and grasped his pistol. In the midst of his fury he beat it twice with all the force he could summon, upon the upturned face that almost touched his own.

She staggered and fell, nearly blinded with the blood that rained down from a deep gash in her forehead; but raising herself, with difficulty, on her knees, drew from her bosom a white handkerchief, and holding it up in her folded hands, as high towards Heaven as her feeble strength would allow, breathed one prayer for mercy to her Maker.

It was a ghastly figure to look upon. The murderer staggering backward to the wall, and shutting out the sight with his hand, seized a heavy club and struck her down.

What reaction does Dickens want from the reader?

How does he get it?

Bill Sykes from a cartoon of the time

Dickens used to give public readings of his novels. He even toured America. The death of Nancy was a favourite reading and members of the audience wept and fainted to hear of her murder.

CHARLES DICKENS'S
DRAMATIC READINGS
AS READ IN AMERICA.

DOCTOR MARIGOLD.

BOSTON:
LEE & SHEPARD, Publishers.
1876.

Towards the end of *Oliver Twist*, Bill Sikes goes on the run. He is chased. He falls from a rooftop as he tries to escape. Read the last passage on page 160 to find out what happens.

Roused into new strength and energy, he set his foot against the stack of chimneys, fastened one end of the rope tightly and firmly round it, and with the other made a strong running <u>noose</u> by the aid of his hands and teeth almost in a second. He could let himself down by the cord to within a less distance of the ground than his own height, and had his knife ready in his hand to cut it then and drop.

Staggering as if struck by lightning, he lost his balance and tumbled. The noose was on his neck. It ran up with his weight, tight as a <u>bowstring</u>, and swift as the arrow it speeds. He fell for five-and-thirty feet. There was a sudden jerk, a terrific <u>convulsion</u> of the limbs; and there he hung, with the open knife clenched in his stiffening hand.

GLOSSARY

noose =
a loop of rope

bowstring =
a cord on an archer's bow

convulsion =
a jerking movement

- Imagine that you are a reporter. The murder of Nancy and the death of Bill Sikes would make a great news story.

- Work with a partner. Your partner should take the part of a witness to Nancy's murder.

- Interview your partner.

- Now swap roles. Your partner is the reporter. This time you are a witness to the death of Bill Sikes.

- Act out this interview with your partner.

DICKENS' LIFE AND TIMES

Look at the timeline of Dickens' life below.
Why do you think he wanted life for poor people to be better?

1812	Dickens born
1815	Napoleon beaten by English at Battle of Waterloo
1823	Dickens lived in prison because his father was deep in debt
1824	Began work aged 11 in a bottle factory
1833	Slavery abolished in England
1835	Became a reporter at the House of Commons
1836	Married
	'Chartists' start their campaign to improve life for poor people
1837	Queen Victoria crowned
1838	Wrote *Oliver Twist*
1840s	These were called the Hungry Forties because life was so bad for poor people
1840	Laws passed to stop child labour
1842	Went to America to speak out against black slavery
1843	Wrote *A Christmas Carol*
1848	Political riots all over Europe
1850	Started a magazine to publish novels in monthly instalments
1858	Started giving public readings of his work
	Left his wife (they had ten children)
1861	Wrote *Great Expectations*
	Start of the American Civil War
1870	Education for all
	Dickens died. Buried in Poets' Corner at Westminster Abbey

DICKENS AND SOCIETY

Dickens lived during the 1800s. In his novels he wrote about things which he felt were wrong with society such as:

  poverty

  slums

  cruelty to children

  dangerous working conditions

  crime

  bad schools

  the legal system

In many of his novels he wrote about the poor, the weak and the lonely people in society. He hoped that conditions for real people like them might improve.

Imagine yourself 1,000 years in the future.

You are writing a story about the terrible life endured by teenagers like yourself in the early 21st century.

Write any 20 lines from your novel.

Use some of Dickens' techniques.

DICKENS AND SOCIETY